TRUE STORI
IN SIX GENERAT

MW00776049

HANNAH'S
Girls

Grace
(1890-1973)

Ruth Vitrano Merkel

REVIEW AND HERALD® PUBLISHING ASSOCIATION
HAGERSTOWN, MD 21740

The Review and Herald Publishing Association publishes biblically-based
materials for spiritual, physical, and mental growth and Christian
discipleship.

The author assumes full responsibility for the accuracy of all facts and
quotations as cited in this book.

This book was
Edited by Penny Estes Wheeler
Designed by Tina M. Ivany
Cover illustration by Matthew Archambault
Electronic makeup by Shirley M. Bolivar
Typeset: Goudy 13/16

PRINTED IN U.S.A.
10 09 08 07 06   5 4 3 2 1

R&H Cataloging Service
Merkel, Ruth Vitrano
    Grace

    1. Seventh-day Adventists—Biography.   2. Seventh-day Adventists—
History.   I. Title   II. Series: Hannah's Girls

                    286.73209

ISBN 10: 0-8280-1953-3
ISBN 13: 978-0-8280-1953-8

Dedication

To my daughters,
Elaine and Marcia,
&
To my grandchildren,
Erin, Benjamin, and Bradley

Contents

Introduction

Quite a few years have passed since Marilla (*Hannah's Girls: Marilla*, Book 2) and her friends graduated from the eighth grade at Sweet Briar School. That happy year had been shadowed by the ever-present news from the War Between the States and her family's concern for her father, who was serving in the Union army. But those long-ago days are past now, and Marilla's life has been busy and happy.

Marilla married her neighbor and childhood friend, Henry Parfitt. They now live in New London, Wisconsin, and are the parents of 10 children.

This third book in the *Hannah's Girls* series finds Marilla's daughter, Grace, excited about winter vacation. Come join in her adventures with her best friend, Margaret. Feel the thrill as they skate on the Wolf River. Watch as Grace learns to stand up for herself and her friends, and learns that life holds pain as well as joy.

This true story is Book 3 of a six-book series.

—*Ruth Merkel*

Hannah's Girls Family Tree

Hannah = Willard Eddy
(1816-1897)

Ann = John Turner   Oscar   Otto
(1883-1897)

Matilda = Henry Padgitt
(1851-1916)

Ida   Annie   James   Daisy   Pearl   Bessie   Hattie   Edwin   John   Grace   Steven   Genevieve   Ruth = Eugene Merkel
                                                Annie Laurie   (1890-1973)   (1981-)

Genevieve   Steven   = Justus Vittone

= Dann Hotelling   Marcia

Elaine   Benjamin   Bradley
(1961-

Erin
(1988-

Generation Three

Grace
(1890-1973)

ERIN'S GREAT-GRANDMOTHER

Some of the people you'll meet in Marilla . . .

🌼 **MARILLA PARFITT:** Grace's mother.

🌼 **HENRY PARFITT:** Grace's father.

🌼 **EDWIN AND JOHN PARFITT:** the two older brothers, closest to Grace in age.

🌼 **DAISY, PEARL, BESSIE, AND HETTIE PARFITT:** Grace's unmarried older sisters still living at home.

🌼 **ANNIE:** one of Grace's married sisters. (Grace learns that Annie has a secret.)

🌼 **MARGARET MURPHY:** Grace's best friend

🌼 **CORLISS MILLIKAN:** a new girl in school. (She came after the winter holidays.)

🌼 **NOLA AND LOLLY:** classmates of Grace. (Troublemakers.)

🌼 **MISS VERA JEAN SIMMONS:** the elementary school teacher.

🌼 **OLD CYRUS:** one of the oldest citizens in New London. (An ice cutter.)

ONE

School's Out

Grace and her classmates ran out of school into the cold December afternoon. Even though the sun was shining, huge, fluffy snowflakes were gently falling, sticking to their caps and mittens.

"Hooray! Vacation time!" Billy and Bert threw their caps into the air and cheered.

"School's out, school's out, teacher let the monkeys out," they chanted.

"Better not let Miss Simmons hear you, Billy Richardson," chuckled Grace, giving him her best Miss Simmons look.

Their teacher frowned at the idea of children comparing themselves to monkeys. Miss Vera Jean Simmons thought that made no sense. No sense at all. And she didn't mind saying so.

Billy grinned. "Puh! I can run faster than Miss Simmons. She won't have a chance to scold me."

"And I can run faster than *you*," Bert boasted, and it was true.

Their schoolmates, Melissa and Tilda, laughed too. Tilda was Billy's sister. She grabbed a handful of snow and ran toward the boys. Bert took off in a flash.

In their typical superior manner, along came Lolly Jones and Nola Hampton, two eighth-grade girls.

"Don't be so childish, Billy, and you too, Bert," Lolly called after the sprinter. "Celebrating just because we're out for vacation. You should value education," she said importantly. Lolly could have been a straight-A student herself, had she not spent so much time thinking about her clothes and planning what she'd wear the next day.

"You're right, Lolly," agreed Nola with a prim smirk. "But you know, boys will be boys."

"I'd rather be a boyish boy than a prissy missy," Billy hollered as he swooped up a large handful of snow.

"Don't you dare throw a snowball at me. I'm wearing my new jacket," Lolly squealed. She and Nola kept walking. But just as they stepped under a large maple tree a thickly-covered branch dropped a huge clump of snow on Lolly's shoulders.

The children howled with laughter. "Billy didn't have to throw a snowball at you, Lolly. Mother Nature did it for him," Tilda giggled.

Lolly and Nola took off on a run.

"Those girls will never change. They've been that way since first grade," Margaret pronounced, nodding her head as if to confirm her own statement. "It's just a matter of fact. Just think, Gracie, now that school's out, we can skate all day if we want. I love winter vacation!" Her eyes sparkled as she thought about the fun they'd have for the next two weeks.

"I love winter, too" Grace said seriously. "It's my favorite time of the year. It's much better than summer with the tornados and storms that come with it. I'll take a blizzard any day."

"And in winter we can sled down Hobb's Hill. I won't break my arm like I did last year," their friend Melissa said. "That was the dumbest thing I ever did!" She laughed at herself even though it hadn't been funny then.

Hobb's Hill was a favorite of the town's children. It was high with a long slope, and was great for sledding and tobogganing.

"We'll watch out for you this year, Melissa," promised Tilda as she linked arms with her classmate.

Grace nodded her agreement, distinctly remembering how she and Tilda had run to Melissa's side after her dreadful collision with the old oak tree. Melissa was a sweet girl and a good friend. They'd all been so scared.

"Next time, Melissa, watch where you're going and just roll off the sled if you see you're headed straight for a tree," suggested Billy who enjoyed giving advice. He really was the smartest boy in class, and very confident. But he was good natured, and he could be funny. All the children liked him.

"You planning on being a gym coach some day and telling folks how to exercise, Billy?" teased Margaret.

"No, Margaret, as a matter of fact I'd like being a doctor," he said with a wicked grin. "I'd even be willing to take out your appendix—and give you a pretty fancy incision, too!"

"Thanks just the same, Billy, but I'll decline your gracious offer." Margaret Murphy was Grace's best friend just as their mothers had been best friends when they were growing up in Liberty, Wisconsin. Cinda Kelly had married Pat Murphy, and Marilla Turner had married Henry Parfitt. Both couples had settled in New London, Wisconsin. Now their daughters played together every day. In the same grade, they were inseparable. Grace was full of fun, yet more quiet and gentle than Margaret. Margaret was outgoing, undaunted, sometimes boisterous and daring. The contrast in their personalities made them quite a pair.

There was nothing that the girls enjoyed more than ice-skating—unless it was jumping rope when the weather was warmer. Winter had come early to New London. *Too* early, the grownups complained. The Wolf River was already frozen. Normally, the river ice was rarely thick enough for skating much before Christmas, but nothing could have pleased the girls more.

Old Cyrus Buchanan, the ice cutter, had announced that the river was solidly frozen and safe for skating. All the children—and the grown-ups, too—relied on Old Cyrus. No one would even think of skating on Wolf River until Old Cyrus gave his approval. Of all people, he'd know the thickness of the ice. Folks said that Old Cyrus was as trustworthy as the day was long. Grace's mother often said that he was "a homespun citizen of sterling character."

He was an immensely tall man with large dark eyes, something like a collie's. Some people thought he looked like a gentle white-haired lion.

The children liked Old Cyrus because he always greeted them with the smile that had carved itself into his wrinkled face. And he said clever, funny things. Grace remembered him telling John and Edwin that he always slept with his boots on so that when he kicked the bucket it wouldn't hurt his toe. When the boys repeated this to their father, his eyes twinkled, and he laughed out loud.

"Yeah, that sounds like Old Cyrus all right. He's as rough as a corncob, but he's a good man—and invincibly optimistic," Papa said with a grin.

It was silly for Old Cyrus to say that he wore his boots to bed so he wouldn't hurt his toe if he kicked the bucket, because "kicked the bucket" was a funny way of saying that someone had died. Grace always giggled when she thought of it.

Grace and her family lived in a two-story house on the corner of Cook and Oshkosh Streets, just up from the Wolf River. Grace was glad she lived near the river. They were so near, in fact, that in the winter when there were no leaves on the trees to block her view, she could see the river from her window seat in the bedroom.

One cold day several years before, Grace's father had taken her down to the frozen river and taught her to ice skate. He explained how she should push a little with one foot while gliding with the other.

She was just a little thing, but her papa thought she was ready to learn. "Try pushing your blade across the ice instead of walking on it, Gracie, and lean on the outside edges," he'd said. He held one of her arms while her brother Edwin held the other. After only two or three spills, she mastered the skill. Before long, her strokes were easy and smooth alongside Papa's.

She remembered feeling so pleased when Edwin proudly declared to their mother, "Gracie is a whiz at skating, Mama. You should see her! She was the littlest one on the river, but she can skate like crazy, and her ankles don't wobble, either."

Grace had shrugged her shoulders and said that it hadn't been hard to learn, but her eyes shone when she looked up at her father. He'd smiled and patted her head. "Gracie, you're definitely from pioneer stock," he'd said. "You're tenacious and tough, and stubborn as well. And you did learn easily, 'tis true." From boyhood, he'd loved ice-skating, too.

Grace was the youngest of Henry and Marilla Parfitt's 10 children. The three oldest were already grown and married—Ida, Annie, and Jim. That left seven still at home—Daisy, Pearl, Bessie, Hettie, Edwin, John, and Grace. The youngest three were avid ice-skaters.

Grace and Margaret had been laughing and chattering as they walked home together. Reaching the corner where their paths parted, they waved and went their separate ways, agreeing to meet later.

In holiday humor, Grace merrily shuffled along through the snow, singing to herself,

> "O Christmas tree, O Christmas tree
> How lovely are thy branches . . ."

She blew little puffs of air into the wind and watched as her breath created small frosty tufts of clouds. Then she reached down and made a snowball, threw it at the trunk of a tree, and watched it crumble and fall. It left the outline of a small round, feathery wreath on the tree trunk.

From the backyard, Edwin saw her coming. "Hi, Gracie. Are you and Margaret planning to skate this afternoon? John and I are going when we've finished our chores. I've just dumped the ashes in the barrel, and now I've got to check the wood supply."

During the winter it was one of Edwin's chores to empty the ashes from all the house stoves once a day. Even though he tried to be careful, he usually got soot on his gloves and jacket as well as some smudges on this face. Sometimes he looked like a chimney sweep all covered with grime. To make the best of it, he'd make funny faces and clown around. The whole family enjoyed his antics. Edwin didn't mind when they laughed at him. The more they laughed, the better he liked it. Edwin had a healthy sense of humor.

"Yes," replied Grace, "Margaret's coming over, and we're going skating too. You do plan to wash your face before you leave don't you, Mr. Ashes?" she teased.

With a grin he elbowed her in the ribs, pushed her aside, and ran into the house ahead of her, then turned quickly and held the door shut. Then he pulled the curtain aside so he could make faces at her through the door window. In a moment his scowl was terrible.

"You be nice to me, Gracie, or I'll get even with you!"

he threatened, hardly able to keep from laughing.

Coming from the storage shed where he'd fed Tip, the family dog, and Bittie, their calico cat, John ran to get in on the fun. Grace and John sometimes teamed up together trying to outfox Edwin.

"Let us in, or we'll huff and we'll puff, and we'll blow your house down!" John bellowed as he and Grace pushed on the door. Suddenly Edwin released his hold and John and Grace tumbled over each other then plunged onto the kitchen floor. Tip danced around them, barking and wagging his tail. But Bittie jumped over the two and headed for her favorite rocking chair near the corner window.

"Sakes alive! What's all the rough housing about?" quizzed their mother. "Have you boys finished your chores? Edwin, I see you emptied the ashes. John did you give Tip and Bittie some clean straw to sleep on? These nights are cold, you know. Then both you boys need to work on splitting some wood."

John nodded his head. "Yes, Mama, they have plenty of nice, clean straw. I fluffed it up a bit, too, and stirred it around." Then going to the kitchen hand pump, he filled the pets' water bowls that were kept on the floor behind the kitchen stove during the winter. In the winter their outside water dishes froze solid.

Tip was a fairly large terrier-shepherd mix, white with a few black spots. He was smart and well mannered. Papa saw to that. Tip learned tricks easily and was devoted to the family. As far as Grace was concerned, Tip could do no wrong.

Bittie was spoiled but sweet. She had an elegant regal look about her. Early on Edwin referred to Bittie as Her Eminence, much to everyone's amusement even if it did suit her.

The small, bewildered cat had appeared one day sitting alone and pitiful under one of the bushes in the Parfitts' front yard. She was just a kitten. Grace spotted her from a window and rushed outside to get a good look. Speaking softly and gently, she'd slowly crept toward the kitten who had let herself be picked up and petted. For Grace it was love at first sight.

The poor thing seemed to have no idea where she was going. None of the neighbors claimed her. Later Papa speculated that someone boating on the river had dropped off the kitten to get rid of her.

"She's such a little bittie thing, I'll take good care of her," Grace promised her parents who somewhat hesitantly agreed. And from then on she was called Bittie.

At night Tip and Bittie slept cuddled together in the storage shed. Daytime, they were allowed in the house as long as someone was home.

"May we go skating, Mama, when we finish our chores?" John asked.

"Yes, but not a moment before. Our supply of wood is getting low," Mother told them as she looked at the wood box in the corner. Then she glanced out of the kitchen window. "The box on the porch needs filling, too."

"No sooner said than done, Madam Lieutenant!" Edwin saluted, and he and John marched out the door like soldiers.

TWO

In Mr. Jennings' Parlor

"*Margaret's coming over* soon, Mama," said Grace. "We want to skate, too. Is that OK?"

"Yes, but first, Gracie—before you take off all your winter duds—would you walk over to Mr. Jennings' with me and help me carry some food? It won't take us long."

Grace gave her a look, but Mama explained. "I want to give him this kettle of soup and some of the bread I baked this morning. We can easily be back before Margaret comes. In fact, along the way we'll stop at her house and tell her that we'll meet her as we come back."

Grace felt sorry for old Mr. Jennings whose wife had died a day or so before, but she wasn't eager to go to his home. She knew that the deceased Mrs. Jennings would be lying in a casket in the front room.

Grace sighed. At times like this she almost wished she wasn't already 12. Growing up had some privileges, but this wasn't one of them! But she squared her shoulders and put on a smile. "Sure, Mama," she said. "I'll go with you."

After pulling a knit hat over her head, Mama put on her long coat and her gloves and picked up the hot kettle by its handle. Even though the soup didn't come to the top, she'd have to be careful that it didn't spill. Grace slipped a small jar of jam into the pocket of her jacket and picked up a loaf of bread that Mama had wrapped in a tea towel.

"This snow *is* beautiful, isn't it?" Mama exclaimed as they carefully went down the snowy steps. Her right hand grasped the step railing, her left hand held the kettle.

"Oh, I love it!" Grace agreed. "I hope someone has shoveled the river so we can skate."

"Someone probably has," her mother laughed. "Everyone knows how you children love to skate." The men in the community assumed the responsibility of keeping the frozen river free of snow, and the older boys willingly pitched in. It was a labor of love.

Side by side, mother and daughter strode down the neighborhood street. They were almost the same height. "Poor Wilma suffered so," Mama mused to her daughter. "I'm glad she is finally sleeping in Jesus. But Clyde will miss his wife dearly. Hopefully this soup will warm his soul and show him our love and sympathy." Mama was very tenderhearted.

Mr. Jennings was not only a neighbor. He was a fellow charter member of their church, and in her young heart Grace truly did feel sorry for him. He was a proper, kind-mannered old gent, altogether different from his wife in temperament and personality.

Mrs. Jennings was not Grace's idea of a nice old lady. In her last years she was pale, peaked, and wrinkled, and for as long as Grace could remember she'd never seen her smile.

Grace walked in silence.

If only Mrs. Jennings had been friendly like Mrs. Eldridge is, she thought. Mrs. Eldridge was her Sabbath school teacher. She loved children and they loved her back. Mrs. Eldridge had a smile for them all, patting the small ones on the head and giving a hug or a warm handshake to the older ones.

No, Mrs. Jennings had never been friendly at all. She was ancient, wrinkled, and always sober. "Crumpled as Methuselah," Edwin had observed. Grace couldn't help but smile to herself even as she walked down the snowy street toward the Jennings house.

And besides, she was ugly. Truly ugly! I know Mama says I shouldn't say that, but how else can it be said? Homely? OK, she was homely.

Grace kept her thoughts to herself, but somehow Mama knew. "Gracie, I know how you felt about Mrs. Jennings, but I do hope that as you grow older you'll grow more understanding and generous in your thinking about the elderly."

Oh, Mama! Grace thought, but she didn't say it aloud.

"Sister Jennings was one of our oldest church members," Mama said unnecessarily.

"I know . . ."

"Well, Gracie, I'll admit it. The poor lady never looked friendly a day in her life."

They could see the Jennings house in the distance. Someone had put a flat black bow on its front door.

"And, Mama," Grace said cautiously, "you'll also have to admit she was very homely."

"Careful now," Mama said, looking at her daughter with a little smile.

The snow was falling faster now. Grace turned her face toward the sky and tried to catch a flake or two in her open mouth.

"You know, Mama, I think that even Mrs. Jennings could have looked . . . well, maybe a little pretty if she'd ever seemed happy. Do you think so?"

Her mother nodded. "It's amazing what happy thoughts will do for your face," she agreed.

Grace hugged the loaf of bread to her chest and changed the subject. "I'm glad it looks like we'll have snow for the holidays."

"I know you are, my snow girl. So I'm glad too."

Mrs. Eldridge met them at the Jennings' front door and cordially invited them in. She and her husband and another couple, the Westphals, had come to be with the recently widowed man. His daughter and son-in-law were there too.

Mrs. Eldridge and Mrs. Westphal were in the kitchen preparing a meal from all the food that had been brought to the home. Mr. Jennings needed to eat, and there'd be plenty for anyone who stopped by to comfort him. The men sat with him and discussed his plans for moving out of the area. His wife's death had been expected, and he'd already decided to go live with his daughter in Fond du Lac.

As they entered the house, Grace saw that, even though it was winter, bouquets of flowers had been placed all around the open casket that stood in the middle of the parlor. With a quiet gasp, she stepped around it and hurried into the kitchen. She just couldn't bring herself to stand and grieve over the departed one. Even though she was 12 years old and almost grown, Grace was afraid of Mrs. Jennings, dead or alive. That's all there was to it.

From the kitchen doorway, Grace politely greeted Mr. Jennings. "Hello, Mr. Jennings. I'm sorry about Mrs. Jennings . . . I mean about her passing and all."

Mr. Jennings came and kindly shook her hand. "Thank you for coming, young lady," he said.

Mrs. Eldridge gave Grace an understanding smile as she slipped her a cookie, squeezing her hand in the process. Grace whispered her thanks. They were special friends. Mrs. Eldridge was personable, friendly, and full of fun.

Eating the fat oatmeal cookie, Grace remembered that just the past Sabbath Mrs. Eldridge had read to them what she called the Golden Rule. It was found in Matthew 7:12: "Whatsoever ye would that men should do to you, do ye even so to them."

Grace remembered that after a slight pause the teacher had continued with an interesting thought. "I sometimes wonder if Peter's personality may have irked some of the other disciples—especially before they'd all felt the Savior's gentle influence. For example, Peter always seemed eager to take care of himself. If someone had asked Peter to pass the salad, would he have helped himself first before passing the bowl along?"

Grace and her young Sabbath school friends had chuckled at that. They nodded to one another.

"Apparently you have seen someone do that. But now, think how Jesus would have reacted." Mrs. Eldridge had paused and looked at each student. "Even if He had not had any salad at all, don't you suppose He would have gladly, unselfishly passed the salad bowl to Peter, giving him all of whatever was left in the bowl without helping Himself first? Isn't that an example of following the Golden Rule?"

Several minutes passed. Grace saw that her mother had slipped her coat back on, so she joined her at the front door. Her mother had stood respectfully by the coffin for a few moments, had sat down and talked with the Jennings' daughter, and now said, "Well, goodbye, Brother Jennings. Remember, we look forward to a wonderful resurrection day when we'll be reunited with our loved ones and friends." She held his old hand between both of hers and looked into his face. "Then there will be no more sickness, nor sadness, nor dying."

"Yes, I know, Sister Parfitt. I know. Thank you for your kindness." Grace heard a tremble in his voice.

"'Bye, Mr. Jennings," she said politely.

"Goodbye, Gracie." He coughed at the blast of cold air, then closed the door behind them. ❁

THREE

When Gracie Whipped the Cream

"All right, Grace, we can head for home," Mama said softly. She pulled on her gloves. "Now then, my little daughter, I was proud of you. You were polite to Mr. Jennings. Part of growing up, you know, is learning to be mannerly in awkward situations. I commend you. Here, let's hold hands so we won't fall. It's slippery." They hurried toward home against the push of the wind.

Down the street they saw Margaret waving and coming to join them, her skate blades flung over her shoulder. She had pulled her blue and white knit stocking cap down over her ears, almost over her eyebrows, so that she had to lean her head back in order to see.

"If your cap came down any farther, Margaret, you wouldn't know where you were going," Grace teased.

"I know, but I'm gonna be warm. Hello, Mrs. Parfitt. Mother is waving her greetings to you," Margaret said, pointing to the window of the house behind her. Mama turned and saw her smiling childhood chum. Cinda Kelly Murphy had been her friend ever since she could remember. Cinda had married Maureen Murphy's brother, Pat, and Maureen was a girlhood chum of both Mama and

Cinda. Grace loved it that their ties with friends went back generations. Mama threw Cinda a kiss and walked on with the girls.

Edwin was waiting for them in the kitchen. Grace just knew he hadn't left because he didn't want to miss her. He gave Grace a comical, crooked grin, his eyes narrowed into little slits, as he stood next to her at the kitchen sink. She was dipping two glasses of water from the bucket, one for herself and one for Margaret.

"So you saw Mrs. Jennings, your favorite shrew," he whispered. "Was she pretty now that her unhappy spirit has left her body, or was it enough to give you the vapors just to look at her?"

Grace could not help but giggle softly. "You are *awful*, Edwin," she playfully whispered back, wrinkling her nose at him. "No, from the brief glimpse I had, Mrs. Jennings did not look pretty. If anything, she was more . . . *homely*." She lowered her voice even more. "Be careful, Edwin, what you say. Mama doesn't want us to be rude about her."

"We did our chores, Mama," pronounced John. "See the wood box? Can we go now?"

"All right, boys, but be back before dark."

Grace quickly pulled on her extra-warm skating clothes, grabbed her skate blades, then she and Margaret were out the door too.

"Have a good time, girls. And remember, Gracie, not too long. An hour should be fine," her mother reminded.

Running down to the river, the girls sat on a nearby log and strapped their skate blades to their boots. Bert and

Melissa saw them and waved as they skated toward them. The ice had been shoveled clean earlier by the men and boys, and it had stopped snowing. Down river Grace could see boys hitting a large flat rock along the slick ice with their sticks and brooms. Little Polly Guthrie was being helped by her father as she learned to maneuver about on the ice. She wobbled on the shiny skate blades, and Grace couldn't help but smile just watching her. Some other girls were skating close to the frozen river's edge. Their mufflers and skirts seemed to float as they skimmed along.

John and Edwin immediately welcomed Grace and Margaret, their skate blades hissing against the ice as they rushed up to meet them. "Wanna play crack the whip?" Edwin asked.

"May I be on the end of the whip first?" Margaret asked excitedly. "It's such fun, even if it's scary."

So they all joined hands and Edwin led them in a row, slowly at first, skating in a wavy line until they built up speed. Then, as the anchor, Edwin stopped and pulled them around. Each one in line pulled on the hand of the next skater, providing increasing speed. Eyes sparkling, Margaret let go. She skimmed along the ice, her hands victoriously stretched over her head, her knees wobbling a bit as she kept her balance. She glided as far as she could, at the end grinning over her shoulder and calling, "How was that?" She wasn't as confident as Grace about skating, but she gave it all she could.

"Hooray, Margaret!" they called back.

"I'm next!" Grace yelled. "I'm at the end of the line."

Billy and Tilda arrived and asked if they could join the fun. "The more the merrier," yelled Edwin. Two more would make an even faster whip line.

Again the friends joined hands, making a long, bright line against the snowy river. "Let's go. Ready or not!" Edwin commanded, and the skaters were off.

When Edwin cracked the whip, Grace hung on until the last minute. Then she shot off like a bullet.

"Oh, oh," cried John, "I hope she doesn't fall."

But Grace sailed swiftly away. With her arms out-stretched, she turned a wide, effortless circle to slow her-self down, then skillfully spinning around, she skated backward toward the group.

"Wish I could skate backward like you do, Gracie," moaned Margaret. "Help me practice before we go home. I need to learn to keep my balance."

"How do you spin so fast?" Tilda wondered aloud. "I'm going to try that."

"Try it slowly at first," cautioned Edwin. "Grace does some pretty daring, remarkable stuff that amazes me. She's got excellent balance for such a slip of a girl."

Melissa grabbed Grace's hand and grinned. "Come skate in the middle of the line with me. I'm too scared to try being on the end of the whip, but I love skating along with the wind so long as I'm in the middle." Her pretty brown eyes sparkled with her laughter.

"Who wants the end this time? Do you Bert? Come on, be a good fellow. Let's see if you can top Gracie's per-formance," John challenged.

"Naw. Let me anchor for you, Edwin. John, you go to the end of the line. I'll whip the daylights out of you!" Bert's boyish face grinned just thinking about it. He and John were cousins as well as friends.

"OK," John laughingly agreed. He wasn't afraid of much.

As the skaters cracked the whip, athletic, young John also hung on until the very last minute. After he let go, he gradually dropped to his knees. They watched as he first settled back on his haunches, then stretched out on his back, down, down until he was lying flat on the ice, his knees bent beneath him

"He's a nut!" laughed Bert.

"No, he's a show-off," Billy countered. "But he's good. I'm too afraid to try his stunts."

"You Parfitt kids can really skate," Tilda exclaimed. "Come on, Gracie, and help us girls practice-skating backward."

When Grace got home, her cheeks were rosy red and her eyes danced. She pulled off her mittens and put them behind the stove on a rack her mother placed there every winter. It was the perfect spot for mittens to dry. Then taking an old towel she wiped off her skate blades and hung them on a peg near the door. Her father had trained the children to take care of their skates so they wouldn't be ruined with rust by hanging them up wet.

"Wow, did we have fun skating, Mama," Gracie happily told her. "We played crack the whip, and I whipped the cream!"

Mama laughed and wagged her head at her youngest

child. She and the older girls were putting the finishing touches on preparing supper, and Mama handed Grace a stack of bowls as she spoke. Grace's sister Hettie had spread the red-checked oilcloth on the table, and placed the saucers, knives, and spoons. They'd have the same rich vegetable soup Mama had taken to Mr. Jennings, with some of her fresh bread. Wisconsin cheese and milk rounded out the meal.

"Oh yes," Grace continued, making sure her sisters were listening too. "Edwin and John said they'll be home soon. They're gonna race with Wesley. You know they don't stand a ghost of a chance to win, but they love trying."

Their teenage cousin Wesley generally raced with the big boys, and usually won. And occasionally, if he happened to be skating while Edwin and John were on the ice, too, he would pretend to race with them. Of course, he could out-distance them, outmaneuver them, out-do their best efforts. But the boys loved the challenge, and they loved Wes.

"Our brothers are such dreamers!" laughed Bessie, placing the big pot of soup on the table. "Wesley is so much taller, and his legs are so much longer than theirs. But they never give up. 'Course, Wes enjoys having them try, and he delights in making them pant like Tip!"

"Let's have some canned fruit, too, shall we?" Pearl asked. "I'll run to the basement and get some." She looked at her mother, who nodded. The hours they spent every summer canning fruit in their hot, steaming kitchen paid off in the winter when there was no fresh fruit to be found.

By the time the boys came back from the river and their father arrived, too, the table was set and the food was ready.

"What huge appetites you have," Papa said with a grin after he'd said the blessing and watched the youngsters shovel food into their hungry mouths. "Exercise and fresh air are invigorating, aren't they?"

"When you were young, you loved to skate, didn't you, Papa?" Grace asked.

Papa's eyes twinkled. "What do you mean, 'when I was young'? I can still skate!"

"Oh, Papa, you know what I mean." Grace rolled her eyes and sheepishly grinned.

"Yes, I loved ice-skating. Like you, I'd skate on anything frozen—even the road in front of our house. The North is a wonderful place to live. All those trips I took to the South certainly convinced me that New London is the place for me."

For many years Papa had worked as an estimator for the lumber barons, both in the north woods and as far south as Alabama.

"I'd rather like to spend one winter where it's a bit warmer," said Hettie, ever the adventuresome girl, "even if it were just to see what it was like not to have snow. Wouldn't it be fun to swim on Christmas day—maybe in the Mediterranean Ocean?"

The boys wholeheartedly agreed.

"If you had lived long ago, Hettie, I'll bet you would have gone to China with Marco Polo," said Edwin, dishing up another bowlful of soup.

"I'm more than content, Henry, to stay right here where we are," said Mama. "It's a blessing for me that you don't work as a lumberman anymore." Papa was now the city assessor and a special police constable. Marilla smiled gratefully at her husband. "You are home year-round now, and that suits me fine."

"Must admit, I like being home, too, Rilla," he answered warmly with that special look in his eyes that he reserved for the mother of his children.

Supper was catch-up time. Mama told the others about her and Grace's visit to Mr. Jennings. Grace and her brothers reported on the action on Wolf River, and the older sisters shared what they'd been doing too. Daisy, working at Milady's Shoppe, often had an interesting story to tell about someone who'd come in, or a new sewing technique she was learning. She thought it was extra fun to work in town for she met so many different people.

After the meal was eaten and the dishes washed and returned to the cupboard shelves, the family gathered in the living room for evening worship.

FOUR

The Piano Box

 Mama, herself, had found the seventh-day Sabbath in the Bible when she was just a little older than Grace. Grace thought that was amazing.

In her heart Grace cherished the story of her mother studying the Bible when she was a young teen. Reading in the Old Testament, she'd discovered the Ten Commandments. To her surprise when Marilla read the fourth commandment she saw that "the seventh day is the Sabbath of the Lord thy God."

The *seventh* day?

Of the week?

That was Saturday!

Her minister told her that this was nothing to worry about, but young Marilla was convinced that God had set aside the seventh day of the week as holy. She determined that if she ever found a church that kept the seventh-day holy, she would join it. And if she had any children she'd teach them to honor God in all parts of their lives—including worshipping on the Bible Sabbath.

So began the journey that led her to the Seventh-day Adventist faith. The history of their family and of the

34

New London SDA Church were closely entwined.

Marilla was a young new mother when Elder H. W. Decker, a Seventh-day Adventist minister, held evangelistic meetings in a tent there in town. Marilla went to the meetings and was both pleased and relieved to hear Elder Decker show from the Bible that *her* conviction about the seventh-day Sabbath was right. She was so excited that she invited her parents, her husband, and his parents to the meetings. As a result, they became baptized members of the New London Seventh-day Adventist Church—all of them, including Grandma Ann and Grandpa John Turner and Grandma Eliza and Grandpa James Parfitt. They were all part of the first congregation of the brand new New London SDA church.

Now sitting in family worship Grace's attention snapped back to the present. A lamp glowed in a window, lighting the snow that lay against the panes. "Let's listen to what Isaiah says about snow," Mama said. "I'm reading from Isaiah 1:18.

> "Come now, and let us reason together,
> saith the Lord:
> though yours sins be as scarlet,
> they shall be as white as snow;
> though they be red like crimson,
> they shall be as wool."

"Isn't that a good text for a winter night?" she said. "And it's a wonderful promise, too." Mama smiled at the seven of her 10 children who sat around the room. Even Tip and Bittie were there. Grace held the cat in her lap and Edwin's hand rested deep in Tip's winter coat.

Papa leaned back in his chair. "We're approaching the end of another year, for 1902 will be here before you know it. Think ahead. What do each of you want to accomplish in the new year?"

"I want to skate better," Gracie blurted out. "I'd love to learn how to spin faster."

The family laughed, and John winked at his little sister.

"I want to be an even better seamstress," Daisy said. "And," she paused, thinking, "I think it would be fun to learn to make ladies' hats."

"I'd like to build my own rowboat someday," said John. "Maybe I could get Old Cyrus to help me." He grinned just thinking about it.

"Sounds like something you'd like to do," Grace said. "You like to putter and experiment with mechanical things! I bet it wouldn't sink, either!"

Edwin joined in. "My goal is to someday own a complete set of Charles Dickins' books for my very own," he said. "Checking them out at the library is far different than having them in my possession. But that may have to wait until I have a job. First I want to graduate from normal school, then when I teach I might be able to finally afford the set."

His father smiled at him. "You continue to do well in your studies, son, and you will be a teacher before you know it. I hear good reports about you from school."

Edwin looked surprised but pleased at the compliment. Everyone murmured their agreement, and Gracie, sitting next to him, patted his shoulder.

"Here is something I learned from my mother when I was a boy," Papa said. "It's a good formula for life. John Wesley—he was a Protestant reformer whom my mother admired—developed this advice. Here's how it goes:

> "Do all the good you can,
> By all the means you can,
> In all the ways you can,
> In all the places you can,
> At all the times you can,
> To all the people you can,
> As long as ever you can."

"Isn't that fine advice?" He looked at his youngest daughter. "And that's just what you did when you went with Mama to see Brother Jennings this afternoon. I'm proud of you."

Pearl leaned over and gently pulled a lock Grace's hair. "Me too," she whispered.

"I think it would be a good idea for each of us to use John Wesley's counsel as our guide for the next year," Papa concluded.

Then Hettie played the piano while the family sang a hymn. Everyone could sing in harmony, and how they enjoyed making music. Bessie, Pearl, and Daisy usually took the lead. Hettie, Grace, and Mother sang alto and Edwin and John carried the tenor. Papa sang bass.

Hettie was by far the family's best musician. She had a lovely low voice, and she could play both by note and by ear. In fact, she could play any song in any key that was needed. Grace could never understand how Hettie did that.

Often Papa played his violin along with Hettie, or just by himself. But Papa didn't play it in the winter when Tip was in the house. At least not during family worship.

Just how Tip became aware of music, no one understood, but since puppyhood he leaned against Papa's or John's legs and howled when they played their fiddles. If the family was singing for fun they usually allowed the dog to croon along with them. However, at family worship his doggie arias certainly distracted their attention.

This night, after prayer, Mama looked at Hettie with a smile. "Do you remember how my mother enjoyed hearing you play, Hettie? She was a fine musician, and I'm sure you inherited her talent. She was as proud as a peacock when you began playing for church."

All the children had heard their grandmother, Ann Turner, play the piano and the pump organ. Grace was only 7 years old when Grandma died, but she lovingly remembered hearing her sing and play at church and in her own home. Other churches often asked Grandma Ann to play for their services too.

"Those fingers of hers were just as much at ease on the keyboard as they were in the kitchen making her delicious chocolate cream cake," Papa recalled.

Grace missed the grandma who had not only seen the stars fall in 1833, but who'd traveled in a horse-drawn wagon all the way from New York to southern Wisconsin when she was just 10 years old. Grandma had told her many stories about that memorable journey.

That must have been a hard trip—no stores, no inns, no railroads along the way for them to use. They were so brave. Probably it was scary, too. Grandma said that there were wolves and other wild critters always nearby.

Grace often had tried to imagine it.

"Do you girls remember how you made your own piano before we actually got one?" Mama asked. The older girls nodded, looking at each other with smiles.

"Yes, Mama, we remember," Daisy declared. "It was a happy day for us when we found that large packing box at the general store and Mr. Wellington let us take it home."

"I remember coloring the black and white keys on the top of the box," said Bessie. "And Hettie, you came up with the idea of crawling under the box and humming loudly while I played the 'keys' with great passion, pomp, and ability—if I do say so myself."

"The neighbor kids came to our concerts," Pearl chuckled. "Do you boys remember? They'd clap enthusiastically, and we'd give our exaggeratedly low bows with such flourish that once Bessie fell."

"I remember one day when Brother Jim first saw and heard us," recalled Daisy. "He stopped and said jokingly, as only Jim can, 'You played like Beethoven today, Hettie.' Pearl nudged the box up, pushed her head out, and said, '*I'm* the music maker, Jim. I *sang* like Beethoven. You give credit where credit's due.' You were so funny!"

FIVE

Papa and the Wolves

Before the children turned to their own evening activities, Grace urged, "Papa, tell us the story about your exciting skate to the Indian camp when you were a boy. I love to hear it over and over again."

Her father leaned back in his chair. He rather enjoyed remembering his terrifying escapade as much as his children enjoyed hearing of it. So with a far-away look in his eyes he told it once again.

"I had skated up the river to the Menominee Indian camp one cold winter afternoon when I was about 10 or 11. The chief was a kind fellow, and I'd become friends with him. His name was Chief White Bear. I had learned enough of their language that I could communicate a bit, at least enough to understand what they were trying to get across. The chief's son could speak better English than his dad, but even his English was on the scant side. However, boys are boys, and we had fun no matter what. I was learning his language, and he was learning mine. That wasn't our main purpose, of course. We just wanted to play.

"Before I knew it, we'd played too long. The sun had just about set, but there was still a bright, rosy glow on the horizon. So I strapped on my skates, pulled my fur cap over my ears, and took off down the river. I went with some degree of haste, I might add.

"I was taken by surprise when I heard a wolf howl way off in the distance. By now I was old enough to have heard every wolf story there was, both from the neighbors and from the Indians. I knew there could be danger if I dilly-dallied, so you better believe I sped up. I didn't know I could skate so fast!

"It wasn't long before I heard another howl, then soon after, a third. No Indian chief had to explain to me that the wolves had picked up my scent and were on my trail. The howls gradually got louder and closer. I wondered how many wolves could there be. As my legs churned down that frozen river it seemed to me that it got dark much sooner than I'd ever known it could.

"With great relief, at last I saw the outline of our barn and house. The white snow lay thick on our roof and the house seemed to glow in the light of the moon. What a welcome sight it was!

"My legs never stopped sprinting until I raced through the door. Father grabbed my arm and asked, 'What's the matter, Henry? You look like you've seen a ghost.' I threw my cap on the floor and answered, 'Didn't see one, but it sure as shooting felt like one was breathing down the back of my neck!'

"After I told Father what had happened, he asked, 'Did you learn a lesson, son?' You better believe, my dear young ones, that I never made that mistake again. Kept my eye on the sun from then on. In fact, to this day I am very much aware of the time of day according to the sun and the sky."

The children sat in thoughtful silence, drinking in the thrill and the suspense of the adventure. Then Edwin spoke up. "Do you really think the wolves could have caught you if you hadn't arrived home when you did?"

"Without a doubt," Papa replied. "Wolves grow vicious, fierce, and reckless when they're hungry. I wouldn't have stood a chance."

Grace shivered, then jumped up and ran to her father, giving him a big hug. "I'm so glad you didn't get eaten up, Papa, or you wouldn't be here with us now."

Her father threw back his head and laughed. "Neither would you be here now, Gracie, nor any other of my children had I been eaten by the wolves."

Everyone laughed.

Her father squeezed her hand. "You're a good girl, Gracie."

Daisy, the oldest sister still living at home, picked up some fabric, her needle and thread, and sat down to sew by the light of a kerosene lamp. She was a seamstress apprentice at Milady's Shoppe in town. It was none other than Julia Dunbar Kelly, Grandma Ann Turner's wagon train friend, who'd opened the shop years before. Now the shop was owned and operated by Julia's daughter, Lucinda Murphy. The friendship between the Parfitt and Murphy families was longstanding.

"You know, Papa," Daisy said thoughtfully, "as many times as I have heard you tell that wolf story it still chills my spine. Grandma Eliza must have had her hands full raising you five kids."

"That she did, Daisy," Papa nodded, "that she did. Considering the cultured environment she had left behind in old England, I've often wondered how she kept her sanity bringing her young 'uns to a new, rather untamed land where we roamed, explored, and wandered on our own much of the time."

"My parents moved their family from an English manor to a log house," Papa added, "but I don't believe they ever regretted it. They loved their new homeland."

As a girl, Eliza had attended the Marl-le-bone Charity School outside London, graduating when she was 14 years old. After that she was employed as a lady's maid by the Squire Ernst family on their large estate in Westcombe, Somersetshire, in southern England. The manor house was lovely and spacious, and the grounds were immaculately cared for. Grandpa James was a gardener on the same estate, and it was there they met, fell in love, and married.

Grace could easily still remember Grandma Eliza's beautiful English accent. She had been a gracious, well-mannered woman. Prim and proper, dainty and attractive, she always carried herself with dignity and with a hint of the old world in her manner.

"The Queen of England couldn't be more regal than Eliza Parfitt," some folks said.

Edwin sat down with a book and began reading. John and Grace went to the table to work on a jigsaw puzzle. Pearl wrote a letter, while Bessie and Hettie sat on either side of their mother as she taught them how to do some fancy crocheting. In her spare time Mama enjoyed crocheting lace for collars, pillowcases, doilies, and handkerchiefs.

The house was quiet and cozy with just the low hum of voices, the occasional crackle of the woodstoves, and the contented hum of the teakettle on the back of the range.

Edwin went to bed earlier than usual. He had been reading Charles Dickens' famous story, "A Christmas Carol," and he slapped his book shut, yawned, stretched, and stood up. "That old man Scrooge was a crotchety soul, wasn't he? Too bad he didn't know Mrs. Jennings. They would have made quite a pair."

"Edwin, mind your manners. It's not polite to speak ill of the dead," Papa advised with a wink.

Sometime after Edwin left the room, frustrated Bessie put down her handiwork. "Oh, fuss and bother," she fretted, once again untangling her crochet thread. "I'm going to stop for the night, Mama. My fingers get all clumsy. Guess I'm just tired." She lit a lamp and climbed the stairs.

Hettie kept on crocheting, but after some time, she, too, put her handiwork in her sewing box. Daisy carefully folded her fabric, and the girls said goodnight to their parents and went upstairs to bed.

John looked over at his father. "Shall I put Tip and Bittie out for the night, Papa?"

When his father waved his hand and said he'd do that, John clambered up the stairs—two at a time.

Pearl stopped her writing and slipped the stationary in the tall secretary. "Come along, Gracie," she coaxed. "I don't want to crawl into bed without you. You're always warm as toast."

"Good night, old Tip," Grace said, patting the dog's head, "see you in the morning. You're such a good doggie. And good night to you, Your Eminence, Bittie."

Tip's tail thumped the floor as he lovingly raised his eyes but not his head. Bittie's eyes narrowed and the tip of her tail switched in an affectionate reply.

Grace and Pearl had the upstairs bedroom on the front side of the house overlooking the big maple tree and the street. Their window had the best view.

Edwin and John had the smallest room at the back of the house. That room had a slanted ceiling. They always said that they were happy they didn't have a large room to keep clean.

Daisy, Bessie, and Hettie shared the largest bedroom.

With the children down for the night, Papa put his feet up on the stool, and Mama leaned her head on the back of her rocking chair. Both parents drew deep breaths and smiled at each other.

"There is something nice about the close of the day," Marilla told her husband. She'd wound up her crochet thread and the ball of thread rested in her lap with the lace she'd just finished. "I must admit that I'm tired. Rocking relaxes me and all but lulls me to sleep, but morning will come too soon."

She took the hairpins from her thick hair and let it fall down her back. "Guess, I'll brush my hair and go to bed." She faithfully brushed her hair 100 strokes every night. It was something she'd done since she was a girl, and she had taught her own daughters to follow her example.

Henry got up and taking Marilla's hand jokingly said, "Too bad that Mrs. Jennings couldn't at least have had pretty hair like yours."

"Henry, you wicked man!" Marilla chuckled. "You are as bad as the children. Edwin loves to tease Gracie about her, because he knows how afraid she was of Sister Jennings."

"I wonder what she'd have looked like if she'd been a happy person," Papa mused. He shook his head. The good Lord loved everyone, and he reckoned that on the judgment day God kept in mind a person's background and their personality. ✿

SIX

Edwin's "Ghost"

Papa pulled on a jacket, called to the pets, and went out to put them in the shed for the night.

Upstairs in their room, Grace and Pearl hung their clothes in the closet and carefully placed their shoes at the foot of the bed. Their father had trained all of the children to put their clothes and shoes in the same place every night, so that if there were any emergency they wouldn't have to search around in the dark for them. "A place for everything and everything in its place," was his motto. Since he was a boy his conservative religious background had shaped his thinking.

"Let everything be done decently and in order," he'd say, "and that can be found in 1 Corinthians 14:40." It was a verse they all learned while very young. The children sometimes groaned and complained that he was too exacting and not flexible enough, but he carefully explained the reasons for his requests, and no one could deny the good sense behind them.

Both Grace and Pearl knelt by their bedsides and said their prayers. The room was cold, and even the rag rug felt chilly to their knees through their flannel nightgowns.

After blowing out the lamp, Pearl joined Grace who

had already hopped into bed. "Oooo, you're so nice and warm, Gracie. You're better than a hot-water bottle. Good night. Sleep tight." She pulled the blankets up and tucked them beneath her chin.

Both girls had almost drifted into peaceful slumber when they felt something bump under the bed and heard a strange sound.

Grace stiffened.

"Stop wiggling," Pearl said sleepily.

"I'm not even moving!" Grace said. Her heart thudded, and she grabbed her sister's hand as whatever it was under their bed bumped their mattress.

"I am the ghost of Christmas Present—the ghost of Mrs. Jennings, ugly Mrs. Jennings," said a strange, squeaky voice. A hand reached up from under the bed and tapped Grace's shoulder. "I'm l-o-o-king," the raspy voice wobbled, "for Graaa-cie Parfitt."

"Pearl!" Grace squealed. "Help!"

Grabbing her sister, she dived totally under the covers.

"Get outta here, Edwin Grant Parfitt, before I strangle you!" Pearl commanded, both humor and disgust in her voice. She jumped out of bed and leaped toward him. "You've read Charles Dickens one too many times."

Edwin quickly wiggled out from his hiding place and for a heartbeat loomed over the bed. He knew he'd better run, but in his hurry he stubbed his toe and fell to the floor, groaning and writhing in pain. "Yeow!" he cried, clutching his injured foot.

Hearing the commotion, the other children came running from their bedrooms. The moon shone brightly through the windows. In its circle of light they saw Edwin on the floor with Pearl standing over him, her hands on her hips. In an instant they understood he'd been up to some mischief.

Then what a rousing, fun tussle they had.

All fear now gone, Grace was laughing and hitting Edwin with her pillow. The sisters were sitting on the floor surrounding their brother, poking fun at the injured culprit. John joined Grace in the pillow fight.

Suddenly, their father stood in the doorway, a kerosene lamp held high in his hand.

"Just what is going on here?" he demanded.

The silence that followed was deafening.

"Are you going to tell me, or shall we start the Inquisition?" They all knew what he meant.

Bit by bit, piece by piece, the story came out while Edwin tried hard not to make a sound. His father stood over him, looking at him quizzically with a hint of a wry smile on his face. Holding down his hand, he helped Edwin stand up.

"This has been enough for one night; for that matter, for one month. You have scared both your mother and me into the middle of next year." Their father frowned, but they could hear the chuckle in his voice. "Now then, everyone back to bed."

Those were the final words from their commander-in-chief, and the children vanished to their own rooms— Edwin limping as fast as he could while holding on to John for support.

"Are you all right, Gracie?" her father asked as she and Pearl climbed back into bed.

"Oh, yes, Papa, I'm fine. Please don't be angry with Edwin. He didn't mean to be naughty. Actually, it ended up being fun."

"Some fun, indeed!"

Grace was anxious that her brother not be scolded. Edwin was a terrible tease, but despite the fact that he could be a rascal, Grace knew that he'd always be her advocate both at home and at school. Yes, they had their moments of squabbling, but they were great friends too. Edwin was her champion, her protector, and she was his loyal, devoted little sister.

"Good night, girls," Papa said. He closed their door, and they could hear his footsteps on the stairs.

Pearl whispered, "I know why Papa didn't get after Edwin. Wait till you see Edwin's toe in the morning. It'll be black as sin. He'll hobble around all day, and he may not try skating tomorrow, either. That's his punishment."

And the girls giggled.

When Papa returned to bed, Mama sighed, "Was bedtime such an occasion for mischief when you were a boy?"

"You forget that I grew up with three brothers, not to mention my sister, Bessie."

"Enough said." She understood completely. Bessie—the daring young girl with enough spunk to ride on a sturgeon fish—undoubtedly was a handful for her parents!

SEVEN

Sleigh Rides

Every day of school vacation was packed with fun. Next to her first love, skating, Grace thought that sledding was pure joy. John and Edwin with their friends, lying belly down on their wooden sleds, sailed down Hobb's Hill. Each one tried to see who could coast the farthest.

Melissa had received a new sled for Christmas.

"Wow," said Grace. The sled was beautiful. She thought it was the finest one she'd ever seen. "Do any of us stand a chance to ride it?" she asked Melissa.

"Oh, sure, but first Bert and I will have a turn."

It was only fair that Melissa's brother had a turn before their friends.

John's eyes lit up as he fingered the metal runners. "Bet she'll fly like the wind, Bert."

Most of the sleds anyone had ever seen were made of wood. When the children waxed the wooden runners, those old sleds flew downhill just fine. But Melissa's sled had a graceful look to it—more like a sleigh. When Grace took her turn on the wonderful sled, Melissa climbed on behind her.

"Don't forget to lean when you want to turn," John told

Grace. "And remember that the sled won't make sharp turns, but it will kind of veer to the side you lean toward."

Bert gave them added advice. "Best to keep a straight course."

"We know, we know," said the girls, anxious to get going, so John and Bert gave them a hefty shove. After that, all Grace could do was hang on. When she felt the sled start to tilt to one side she yelled, "Lean!" As they shifted their weight, the sled shifted, too. Gaining speed, the marvelous new sled seemed to leap as it went over slight bumps in their path. With every bump the girls shouted and laughed all the more. Snow blew into their faces, but they just turned their heads and blinked it out of their eyes. Wind whipped their hair and stung their cheeks. The trees and shrubs on the side of the hill flew by in one long blur.

Exhilarated, they reached the bottom of the hill and gradually the sled slowed to a stop. The girls rolled off and lay on their backs, looking up at the sky. They were covered with snow, but they didn't care. Even the icy snow jammed into the top of their mittens, stinging their wrists, didn't bother them.

"That was great!" Grace's eyes beamed as she rolled to her side and grinned at her friend.

"It was! Let's do it again."

So they got up, and pulling the sled behind them, started their long ascent to the top of the hill. Margaret and her brother Ray were waiting for them.

Of course, Margaret was given a turn on the now-famous sled.

Melissa was a celebrity that afternoon.

Before they left for home, Ray Murphy asked Edwin and John if they'd like to go for a sleigh ride sometime.

"Really, Ray, you have a sleigh now?" Edwin asked. He grabbed Ray's arm in surprise. They were classmates and good friends.

"Yeah, Pa got that old one from Mr. Jennings who's going to live with his daughter, you know." Over the past weeks Simon and Ray had worked hard on the sleigh, rubbing down its runners, repairing loose parts, and shining it up. "It looks real good, too, even if it's old," Ray told him. "It's sturdy, and my Pa said we could use it. Would any of you like to go?" Ray's eyes danced. He was eager to take out the sleigh, and it would be much more fun if friends were along.

"How soon?" Edwin questioned.

"Does tonight sound good?"

It sounded great to Edwin. He suggested that Ray and Margaret go home with him and his brother and sister so they could ask if it was OK to go sleighing.

Mama was surprised to see them all. "Come on in," she told the company. "What brings you here? Everything all right?" She laughed and gave Margaret a hug. "No mischief planned?"

"Everything's just fine, Mama," Edwin told her. "Ray just wondered if we wanted to go for a sleigh ride tonight. Did you know that Mr. Murphy bought old Mr. Jennings' sleigh?"

"Why, how nice of you to ask, Ray. I guess I did hear about the Jennings' sleigh, but I gave it no further thought." She nodded. "A sleigh ride would be fun, and I know you'll be careful." She reached out and tapped Ray's shoulder. "You keep shooting up like a beanstalk, Ray, and you'll soon be as tall as your brother Simon."

"That's what Ma says," replied Ray proudly. "Well, I am almost 15, so I guess it's OK to start growing. Sure has taken me a while."

They all laughed with him and John went up and stood close to Ray so that he could measure his own height by comparison.

Hettie and Bessie couldn't help but hear the conversation and came running from the next room.

"How about us, Ray? Will you take Pearl, Bessie, and me, too?" Hettie's eyes shone with excitement.

"Sure. We'll just have to take turns. The sleigh can hold four or five of us easily if we squeeze together."

Grace jumped up and down with eagerness. "Oohhh, I can hardly wait." She and Margaret waltzed around the room.

"We'll go home now and tell Pa," Ray said. "Be sure to dress real warm. We have a couple buffalo robes, but you should bring blankets."

"Or a metal foot warmer, if you have one," Margaret said. A foot warmer filled with coals from a hot stove put off a nice warm heat.

Just as Ray opened the door to leave, Papa walked in. "Hello there, me boy. Good to see you," He shook Ray's hand then turned to Margaret with a welcoming smile.

"Oh, Papa," began Grace, "Ray is taking us for a sleigh ride."

"So Pat Murphy has done wonders with Jennings' old sleigh, has he?" Papa said with a grin. "I'll bet you boys have had fun with your father getting it all gussied up, haven't you? But it was hard work, too, I'm sure."

"Yeah, it sure was," Ray replied, "and Pa made us be pretty careful when we sanded and painted. He told us that whatever Pat Murphy did, he did right, so he wanted his sons to follow his example. It was fun, though."

"You'd best skedaddle home now," said Mama to the Murphy kids. "Give my regards to your mother. See you later."

As their friends left, the children surrounded Papa, each of them wanting to tell about their exciting plan. "You'll have fun," he told them. "It's been a while since I've been in a real sleigh. Seems like most folks just put runners on their wagons and get around in the snow that way. But a real sleigh is nice. What a high time it ought to be."

And sure enough, it was. Just as supper ended, Simon, Ray, and Margaret pulled up in front of the house in their sleek, shining sleigh. Lanterns hung from brass hooks at the front of the sleigh. Their light gleamed in the darkness, casting halos of warm light in the snow. Buffalo robes covered the old leather seats, ready to provide protection and warmth to the passengers.

"You must have polished the daylights out of this ancient sleigh," Papa noted with humor as Grace and Margaret ran around inspecting the fine old vehicle.

"Yeah, we polished all right, but it won't stay that way for long," said Ray.

"Pulleeze, Sy, can we go first?" Grace would have dropped to her knees if she thought it would have helped.

"Well, I told Edwin and John they could be on the first run," Simon explained, "but . . ." He rubbed his chin and playfully hesitated. Turning to his younger brother he said, "Do you think Gracie and Margaret might fit?"

Ray nodded and helped the girls up and into the sleigh.

Mama came out on the porch. "Here's a warm soapstone and some extra horse blankets."

"Thanks. When we return, we'll give you and Mr. Parfitt a ride. Any of the older girls are welcome, too," Simon said to Mama.

When everyone was tucked in securely Simon patted his horse's big black shoulder and adjusted the blanket. He wanted the horse to be comfortable, too. Barney snorted, tossed his head and shook his mane which started the sleigh bells jingling and tingling. Snuggled under blankets, the girls giggled. Then Simon climbed aboard and clicked, "Giddy up!" They were off.

Going straight down Oshkosh Street, they then turned and followed the road along the side of the river. The sky was cloudless and clear, and it seemed the whole town was out skating. The high, bright moon cast a white glow over the river and skaters. Flames from the warming fire on the riverbank glowed merrily, giving the scene a fairytale look.

Simon slowed the horse as they drew near to town.

The hotel and a few shops were open. Grace and Margaret waved and shouted to everyone they saw. "Hello, Mrs. Bowman! Happy New Year, Mr. Lowry! Hello, Mrs. Talbot! Hi there, Mr. Richardson. Hi, Billy!"

"Did you see the look on Billy's face when he saw us?" Grace asked with an ear-to-ear grin. Margaret nodded and laughed.

"Evening, Mr. Pettibone, and you, too, Mrs. Pettibone," Grace called as she waved.

"Aren't you a little forward, waving to the president of the bank?" Simon chuckled. "Or are you personally acquainted with him?"

"I just recognized them both and decided to say hello. 'Least I didn't say 'Evening Lionel and Lydia.' Now that would have been *brash*, as Mama would say."

"We'd better not meet too many other dignitaries, Grace," Ray warned, "or you'll fall overboard."

"He's right, Gracie," said Edwin. "It's best to sit still."

"But I want to see everything and everybody." Grace settled back and tried to restrain herself.

"I rather think you girls want everybody to see *us*," laughed Simon.

Now on the other side of town, Grace was enchanted with the scenery. The lanterns swung with the motion of the ride, sending shimmering streams of light across the snow. Here and there a rabbit zig-zagged ahead of the sleigh. An owl hooted from the trees, and Simon pointed out a deer standing as if frozen along the edge of the tree line, its silhouette barely visible. Then it darted away and vanished.

"Isn't this fun? I'm so glad old Mr. Jennings sold his sleigh." Margaret was enjoying herself, too. It was a quiet, moonlit night, and the young people were in a holiday mood. The boys had a running conversation going, but sometimes they grew completely silent, charmed by the beauty around them. Tall evergreens shimmered in their covering of ice and snow, and the only sound they could hear was the crunch of Barney's hooves and the *swoosh* of the sleigh's runners.

Simon clicked to the horse, and they picked up speed. The sleigh rocked gently, and Grace squeezed Margaret's hand.

As the boys laughed and talked, Grace whispered to Margaret that her mother had warm, mulled cider waiting for them when they got home.

"Really? Ooooo. I love cider." Margaret clapped her mittened hands. "I like cider even better than hot cocoa."

When the road leveled out, Simon turned the horse, and they dropped down the slight incline onto the frozen river. As they headed back, Ray started singing, so everyone enthusiastically joined in:

"Jimmy crack corn, and I don't care,
Jimmy crack corn, and I don't care,
Jimmy crack corn, and I . . ."

Their young voices echoed in the cold, still air.

Soon they saw lamplights from the homes in town welcoming them back. Smoke rose from chimneys, and the crisp air was filled with the fragrance of burning wood.

More sleigh bells told them that another sleigh was approaching, and they all strained their eyes to see if they could recognize the riders. Everyone waved as they passed, and only then did they recognize their cousin Wes with a young lady.

"Why that was Emily Crockett, Palmer and Lorena's daughter," Ray said in surprise. Palmer Crockett owned the sawmill in town.

"Wes with a girl! Of all things," John mumbled.

"Well, he's old enough to take a girl for a sleigh ride," Simon chuckled. "I just didn't know he was aware that girls existed."

"How romantic," Margaret giggled, elbowing Grace.

"Humph," said John. "Wes could have had more fun if he had taken me along with him, 'stead of a girl!"

Everyone laughed. "Yeah, sure, John. You and Wes in the sleigh, alone together on a moonlit night. That would be some fun," Simon teased.

When they arrived home everyone had a cup of warm cider, and gathered around the stove, enjoying the fire's welcome warmth. Then Pearl, Bessie, and Hettie—laughing and all talking at once—left for their turn in the sleigh.

Grace heard Pearl say, "Won't Daisy be disappointed that she isn't here for the sleigh ride?"

"No, she'd rather be sitting next to Gustave. That's just as thrilling for her," laughed Bessie.

Gustave Maas was Daisy's beau, and that evening Daisy had accepted an invitation to supper at his parents' house. Grace thought Gustave was wonderful, and she could see why Daisy had fallen in love with him.

They were still standing at the fireplace, their reddened hands stretched toward its warmth, when Mama asked if they'd like to put together a puzzle.

"Oooo, yes," Margaret said. "I love puzzles." So the girls settled down at the table and chattered away as they worked and sipped their hot drinks. Edwin read. John sat on the floor with Tip near the stove, holding Bittie in his lap.

When the sisters returned, Simon suggested that Papa and Mama might like to take a spin.

"Of course we would. Come along, Marilla, my wife. I'll help to keep you warm!" Papa's eyes twinkled and Marilla playfully nudged his arm as she wrapped her scarf around her neck.

Grace danced around her parents. She didn't say a word, but her eyes begged the question she didn't ask.

"Oh, come along, Gracie, we'll make room for you." Her father smiled down at her. "Would you like to join us, too, Margaret?"

"No, but thanks. I'd rather do the puzzle." She was working intently now with Hettie and John at the table.

So off went Grace for a second sleigh ride. It was a night she would never forget. Climbing into bed, she wondered if she could ever get to sleep. But when she did, she dreamed of moonlight and jingling bells, snow-laden trees and warm, mulled cider. ❄

In Milady's Shoppe

After vacation, it was back to school as usual. Grace was happy to see all her classmates again. A new girl had joined them, too—Corliss Milliken. Her father had taken a job with the city's public works department. Corliss wore her blond braids wrapped around her head. *It's like a halo, but a little old-fashioned,* Grace thought as she looked at the girl's fair, round face. Corliss was as quiet as a mouse. At recess, Grace and Margaret invited her to play with them. She hesitated at first but then shyly joined in a game of tag.

"She's a dainty little thing but skittish as a kitten," Margaret remarked later.

"Well, wouldn't you be shy coming to a new school in the middle of the year?" Grace asked. "Well, maybe not, knowing *you,* Margaret." They both laughed.

"She has a slight accent when she talks, and I saw Lolly and Nola look at her kinda skeptical like. Then they walked off and snubbed her." Margaret looked disgusted.

"Oh, well, Lolly Jones and Nola Hampton don't cotton to too many of us, anyway," Grace said. "Corliss' accent is German. She told me that in her home they speak both German and English. Her dad's American, and her mother was born in Germany. That's where the family has lived for the last five years. They just recently returned to Wisconsin. I'm sure Lolly and Nola think her hairdo is old-fashioned, too. Anyway, I think it's silly to make fun of someone because they're not *fashionable*." Grace turned up her nose and minced across the room to imitate the way Lolly sometimes walked.

Margaret shrugged. "Corliss' clothes are clean, even if they're not fashionable."

"Well, my dresses have been tucked, shortened, and lengthened more times than I can count! I wear my sisters' hand-me-downs. I hardly ever have new things."

Daisy did wonders with the much-worn clothes of Grace's older sisters. Where the material wore thin, she'd appliqué a flower in a contrasting color. When a let-down hem showed the previous hem line she'd cover it with rick-rack or a ruffle. And sometimes she took a dress completely apart and put it together in a whole new way.

Margaret told Grace that she was lucky that Daisy was so handy with a needle and thread. Margaret's mother often said that Daisy was the best apprentice she'd ever had.

The weeks passed and Corliss became more at ease with the girls near her age and grade. Still she remained quiet and a little reserved. She wasn't the quickest student, nor the slowest. Of course, Lolly and Nola ignored her completely.

One afternoon Margaret suggested that they take Corliss to Milady's Shoppe and show her around.

"Do you think your mother would mind, 'long as we behave?" Grace wondered.

"She won't care," Margaret replied. She grabbed Corliss' hand. "Come on."

Margaret and Grace had never been allowed to play in the shop, but if they were quiet and mannerly they could enjoy a few moments looking around. Milady's Shoppe was well known for its excellence in dressmaking and tailoring, and both local women and those from nearby towns came there to shop for cloth and "notions." The two wide showroom windows were kept smudge-free. The window displays were always stylish and attractive, and the store itself was bright and cheery.

The three friends walked through its doorway. Just inside the shop, they stopped and Corliss let out a low gasp. Before her eyes were shelves holding bolts of fabric—gingham, calico, flowered and plain cottons, lovely plaid wools, silk, and airy netting which Daisy had said was used for weddings. On a nearby rack spools of sewing and crochet threads in a rainbow of colors were neatly stacked next to skeins of yarn. Corliss pulled her gaze from the threads to see sewing needles, quilting needles, knitting needles, and crochet hooks. Bonnets, gloves, and lace fans were displayed on a small table, and hats trimmed with flowers and veils stood on another.

Corliss stood dumbstruck.

"Oh my, I've never seen such a wonderful store," she whispered. "How I'd love to work here when I grow up."

Daisy and two other girls worked as apprentices in the back fitting room of the store where they measured, trimmed, cut, and sewed, all under the careful supervision of Mrs. Murphy. Early in her training Daisy had surprised both herself and Mrs. Murphy when she'd learned to cut out a dress without the aid of a pattern.

"Daisy is a natural," Mrs. Murphy had told Mama. "She just seems to understand graceful lines and the flow and drape of the fabrics."

First Daisy sketched whatever she planned to make, and then by using precise measurements she could cut the fabric and create a beautiful gown, dress, skirt, or blouse. In time, Daisy knew, she and Gustave would be married. She loved imagining their wedding and enjoyed looking at the few fashion magazines and pattern books which Mrs. Murphy ordered from New York. Every stitch in her wedding dress would be made with love.

Grace and Margaret took Corliss over to the two long mirrors that stood near one wall. The girls preened and primped, imagining themselves wearing beautiful gowns with long gloves up to their elbows, and high-heeled shoes.

Margaret said in a low whisper to Grace, "May I help you, madam? Have you seen our beautiful fabrics from France and these soft wool shawls direct from Scotland?"

Smiling graciously, Grace quietly replied with an affected accent, "Please, do you have some Irish linen in powder blue?"

Corliss giggled and joined in the fun. Then they quietly and politely left the store after thanking Mrs. Murphy and her sales clerk, Mary Ellen Chamberlain.

In Daisy's estimation, of all the ladies in New London Mary Ellen had the best taste in clothing.

"It's not that she acts superior or puts on airs," Daisy had told Mama. "She knows what looks good on her, and she wears her clothes well." Not even Lydia Pettibone—who had lots of money—had more style. Lydia did have more money to spend on the latest fashions, but she didn't have more flair.

Grace had edged close to Mama and Daisy so she could hear every word of their conversation. Mama agreed with Daisy. "Mary Ellen is a working girl. She doesn't come from wealth or from nobility, but she has excellent taste in clothing and in her conduct."

After that, whenever Grace happened to see or meet Mary Ellen, she took note of the way the young woman walked and talked, how she combed her hair, and how she spoke to those she met or waited upon in the Shoppe.

That's how I want to be—polite and tasteful. Even if I don't have lots of money, at least I can look nice, have good manners, and be neat and clean.

Sometimes when Grace was by herself, she practiced walking slowly and gracefully around her room. Holding the mirror, she'd pull her hair back and up, turning this way and that to look at herself. Her sisters all told her she had the prettiest hair in the family and in her heart of hearts Grace liked to think that was true.

Grace knew that her family didn't have a lot of money, but they were happy and satisfied with their lot in life. Oh, of course, the sisters sometimes complained that they didn't have many dresses. Sometimes one would ask the other, "Well, what shall I wear to church today? My *best* alpaca?"

(Alpaca was a thin material that contained wool from alpaca, animals with a soft fur that lived in Peru. Their question was a joke, for the Parfitt girls only had one alpaca dress each.)

But their mother—in her own much-worn outfit—would give loving counsel. "If you behave half as nice as you look, girls, you'll do well." Early in childhood Grace learned that manners were more important than clothes.

That evening during supper Grace told the family about taking Corliss to Milady's Shoppe. "I don't know if she'd ever been in a dress shop before," Grace added. "She was so excited about everything."

Edwin said that Corliss' brother, Caleb, was in his grade. "I like him," he said. "He's smart, and he's nice. He can add columns of several figures in his head and come up with the answer before I can using pencil and paper!"

"I think he's quite good looking," Hettie mused.

"Oooooo," teased Edwin and John immediately.

"Are you sweet on Caleb?" John teased, drawing out the word "sweet."

"Yeah," said Edwin. "Have you set your cap for him?"

"Oh, go on with you both," Hettie laughed. "I think he's nice. He's my age, you know, but he's behind in school because of their stay in Germany."

"Is he your boyfriend?" asked Grace, her eyes wide with curiosity.

"Yes, honey," Hettie said gently. "He's a boy and he's a friend. But he's not my beau. There is a difference, you know."

NINE

Annie's Secret

The school year was passing swiftly, or so it seemed to Grace. And so were the snow and ice, much to her regret. The snowfalls didn't come so close together, and when it did snow, it melted quickly. The river was almost thawed, and today the air was definitely warmer.

Grace stood at the kitchen window, a dishtowel in her hand. She was watching an early robin hop from place to place in the sparse green grass. Now he stopped, cocked his head, and darted forward. A moment later she laughed out loud when the bird hopped away with a worm dangling from his beak.

"So that's what it means by 'the early bird gets the worm'," she said aloud to herself. This silly robin should still be in the South, but here he was, fattening himself on worms and maybe even starting to build a nest. She'd have to be on the lookout for a Mrs. Redbreast.

She pricked up her ears at the sound of a horse and buggy in front of the house. When she heard it stop she put down the plate she was drying and went to see who it was. To her delight it was her sister Annie.

Grace was always glad when her Annie came to visit.

Eighteen years older than Grace, she was married and a young mother. And Annie and her husband, Reynolds Stern, had a young son that Grace thought was a cutie. Dell's blue eyes sparkled, and his little round face was always smiling. He seemed more like a little brother to her than a nephew. Dell loved her too, and whenever they were together he was right on her heels. She'd sweep him up in her arms, hold him on her lap, and clap his little hands, saying:

> "Pattie cake, pattie cake, baker's man
> Make me a cookie as fast as you can
> Roll it and roll it, and mark it with 'D'
> And throw it in the oven for Dell and me!"

Oh, how he giggled when she threw his arms wide to throw the cookie in the oven!

Calling up the stairs to let her mother know they had company, Grace watched as Reynolds carefully helped Annie down from the wagon. Grace ran out to get Dell then followed the little boy's parents into the house.

Mother and Annie were kissing hello. Annie gave Grace a hug, and Reynolds took Dell from her arms. He said they were going to see "Grandpa Henry" at the boathouse by the river. Then with a wave at Grace, they were gone.

Well, humm, thought Grace, *What's he doing holding Annie's arm and helping her into the house like? She didn't say she was sick or anything when she came in and hugged me.*

Back in the kitchen Grace continued to dry the dishes

v-e-r-y s-l-o-w-l-y, her head cocked toward the front room. She was trying to hear the conversation. Only able to catch a word every now and then, she knew better than to stand in the doorway, dishtowel and bowl in hand, listening.

She could see Annie sitting and rocking, her head resting on the back of the tall chair. Mother sat next to her holding her hand. Their voices were low, but their faces didn't seem to show fear or alarm. So what was all this whispering and murmuring about?

At last the dishes were dried, but Grace still did not know what the secret was. She carefully joined her mother and sister, and the topic of their conversation was guardedly changed. Annie smiled at Grace and squeezed her hand. "And how are you, my little sister? You're growing taller—and prettier—every day. I must say Grandma Eliza was right. You *are* a bonny lass. And you carry yourself gracefully for one still young. You named her right, Mama!"

Grace flushed under the smiling appraisal and glance of approval from her big sister. Mother nodded. Grace knew they were sizing her up with pride.

She drew a deep breath and smiled almost with embarrassment. Running to the door, she said, "I'm going to see if I can find Papa, Reynolds, and Dell down at the river."

Later that evening Grace hesitantly approached her mother. She wanted to know what was going on.

"Mama, is Annie sick?" she asked. "She didn't seem so, but I thought she looked worried and pale."

Mother put her arm around Grace's shoulders. "No, my dear, Annie isn't sick. But I should have known that nothing would get past your sharp eyes." She laughed. "Annie just came to me for some advice and comfort."

Now Grace was really puzzled. "You see," Mother went on, "Annie is in the family way, and right now—early on—she's been quite sick to her stomach. She just needed a little comfort and counsel."

Grace's ears immediately picked up the words "family way." She knew what that meant. Of course, that subject was never openly discussed in front of children. It was hardly even discussed among adults except for grown women, and even they always lowered their voices.

Grace stammered excitedly, "You—you—you mean Annie is going to have a baby? Oh, how wonderful. Dell is such a cutie. He'll love having a new baby around!" Grace almost danced a jig right there in the living room.

"Now, Gracie, my dear," said Mother, "you just keep your ears open but your pretty mouth shut. Annie is not making this known just now, so we'll not speak of it to anyone. Let's not steal her thunder—you know what I mean. Let her spread the good news when she chooses, not when we choose."

Grace felt herself grinning from ear to ear. It was wonderfully exciting to have such a secret, but she wouldn't even be tempted to share it. It was enough to know it herself. 🌼

TEN

Birthday Girl

Before she knew it, spring had burst upon them. Grace didn't complain, though. The warmer weather brought out the buds on trees, a carpet of green grass, and the yard filled with birds who'd flown up from the south where they had wintered. And spring brought April, the month in which she was born.

The morning of her birthday, Grace awoke feeling good. Somehow it seemed that everything was right and nothing was wrong. She felt glad to live in a free country and in the beautiful state of Wisconsin. She felt proud of her government, of her church and her family. She felt proud of everything.

The day before, Miss Simmons had been inspired while teaching American history. Grace and the other children had caught her spirit. "Be proud to be Americans, children!" she'd said, and those words rang in Grace's ears as she lay in bed looking at the ceiling. The springtime sun streamed through the windows and cast lacy shadows on the walls.

Every day before their classes began Miss Simmons had her students repeat the pledge of allegiance to the flag of the United States. She told them that a fellow named

Francis Bellamy had written the famous words when he was, himself, in grade school in 1892. That was within their own lifetime! Miss Simmons had the children place their hands over their hearts when they repeated the beautiful words of the pledge to the American flag. And somehow yesterday the walls of the classroom had seemed to ring with patriotism.

As Grace jumped out of bed she heard a robin chirp its greeting to the morning sun. She looked out the window and there sat the bird on a branch almost within reach. She hurried to get ready for school.

It was a long day in the classroom. Not that she didn't have fun with her classmates. Melissa drew a funny picture for her of a girl wearing a birthday crown. At recess Margaret led a group in singing Happy Birthday. And Corliss squeezed her hand and whispered her best wishes.

But it was the family party in her own home that Grace was waiting for. And then school was out and she was home. Her mother and sisters shooed her out of the kitchen. She was to have no part in preparing her birthday dinner. And now they were all singing:

> "Happy birthday dear Gracie,
> Happy birthday to you!"

Grace smiled at the big group seated around the dining table. Her eyes sparkled like the candles on her birthday cake. *In a few months there will be another little face at the table—if Annie comes, that is.* A faraway look filled

Grace's eyes. She couldn't wait for the baby to come. Of course, most people didn't even know about it. She felt sure that neither Edwin nor John knew yet.

"Wake up, Birthday Girl!"

Bessie's voice brought her back to the party. For after supper her mother and Bessie had gone to the kitchen. Here was Bessie with the luscious-looking chocolate cream cake and its glowing candles.

With an exaggerated stride and a wide smile, Bessie sashayed up to Grace's chair. "I helped Mama with the frosting. Isn't it pretty! Do you like it?" she asked.

Grace gazed at her birthday cake with glowing eyes, then smiled at her sister. "Ohhh, it's really fancy, and I love it!"

"Now take a big breath and see if you can blow out *all* those *many* candles!" joshed Edwin. He winked at his younger brother. "Shall we spank her, John?"

"You do, and you'll have me to contend with," threatened Bessie as she grabbed Grace in a playful, pro-tecting hug. Bessie was 10 years older than Grace and was always ready to protect her. When school started next fall Bessie was going for Battle Creek, Michigan, where she would train to become a nurse at the famous Battle Creek Sanitarium.

"If I hear that any of you are mean to Gracie while I'm gone, I'll get even with you when I come home!" Bessie warned with a smile. She squeezed her little sister even tighter. "I'll miss all of you so much. Please write often," she begged. "I think I'm already beginning to have cold feet about being so far away from all of you."

Grace threw her arms around her sister. "We'll write regularly, Bessie, and we won't forget you."

"Well, let's have that chocolate cream cake. I'm ready!" John said, patting his tummy and licking his lips. He loved to eat, especially dessert.

"John Dudley Parfitt," said Grace, "I do believe you have the biggest appetite of anyone I know. You'll grow up to be tall, wide, and huge, and we'll have to design a house for you with extra-wide doorways."

Everyone laughed. John loved to tinker and putter with clocks and wheels and springs and mechanical things. When he was stumped he always consulted Grace who also enjoyed being challenged. Together, they usually could fix anything—anything simple, that is. One time, working together, they took a clock completely apart and put it back together. It worked, too!

"I'm an inventor, Gracie, and you're an inventor's wife. We're both clever," they had chuckled together.

After blowing out her candles, Grace helped her mother cut the cake. First she gave a big wedge to both her mother and father. Then she cut and passed a slice to each one. A special guest that day was Gustave, Daisy's fiancé. Everyone in the family was taken with the mannerly, courteous, and pleasant Gustave. He was tall and slender with brown, wavy hair and a good sense of humor. Grace thought he was marvelous, and he returned her admiration. Seeing him with Daisy appealed to her young, romantic heart.

Grace handed Gustave a generous slice, and he winked his thanks.

"I figured you need a large piece." She leaned across Daisy and whispered in his ear. "You're so lean and lanky."

He grinned, happy to be part of their family. "I'll just send it down to my hollow leg," he said.

Daisy patted her lips with a napkin. "Ummmm, simply delicious, Mama." She dreamily closed her eyes and wagged her head. "You know, this is my *favorite* cake. Let's have this at our wedding reception, Gustave."

He nodded and placed his arm around the back of Daisy's chair. "That's fine with me," he agreed with fondness in his eyes.

He's none other than Prince Charming himself! Gracie thought.

"It's from an old family recipe," Mama told Gustave, "and it's always been a winner. Daisy's Grandma Ann Turner made it famous by often making it for church dinners or picnics. I remember her telling me that her own mother—Great-grandma Hannah Eddy—was the best cook on the wagon train. That pioneer woman once baked a cake in a Dutch oven over an open camp fire. Now that's talent!"

"Can I have another piece, please Mama?" begged John who had, with a few huge bites, already finished his slice.

"There's only a little left, John. Let's save that for the birthday girl."

"OK," he replied, but disappointment was written all

over his face. "For *my* birthday, please bake two cakes for me. Pulleeze!"

John's birthday was just two weeks away, and he could hardly wait. He was always active and loved sports. He also had a healthy appetite.

"That's a splendid idea—*two* cakes for your birthday," Edwin agreed.

"What makes you think you're gonna get some of it? I'm gonna eat the entire second cake all by myself." John laughed, but they all could see he meant every word, and they knew he'd surely try.

Mama smiled at Gracie, her mind years away. "Just look at you, Gracie," she said from her chair next to Papa. "You have grown quite a bit in one year. Do you remember, Henry, how when she was first born the doctor told us to take her out in the sun as much as possible? She was a wee little one, I'll never forget. Guess he just didn't know how strong the members of our Turner-Parfitt family can be. You're as fine, fit, and healthy as any young girl I know. Happy birthday, honey."

She reached toward her youngest child, and Grace slipped into her arms. Mama drew the birthday girl's slender body close to the side of the chair and gave her a hug and a kiss.

Grace returned the hug. "You're the best mother in the whole, wide world."

Then she stepped to her father and gave him a resounding kiss on the top of his head. Everyone laughed. She looked at Papa with a grin, and he gave her a quick wink.

His slender daughter had his blue-gray eyes—eyes that easily danced with laughter or flashed with disapproval. Unlike her mother's straight hair, Grace's dark brown locks were naturally wavy. Though they tumbled over her shoulders, they were easily manageable. Her chin had a gracious curve, and her mouth was sweet. She was a shyly charming, but determined girl. Everyone said Grace was the child who most resembled both sides of the family.

"The Parfitts and the Turners have surely joined together when young Gracie was born," grandmother Eliza Parfitt often said. "I can clearly see both her mother and her father when I look at her sweet face." Grandma had smiled as she cupped Grace's chin in her hand and placed a soft kiss on her forehead.

"You're a bonny lassie. Yes, a fair, winsome lass, my sweet child." And Grandma's arms had lovingly surrounded her youngest grandchild.

❧

Grace remembered Grandma Eliza with great affection. She'd always loved hearing Grandma tell stories about her beloved old England where she was born and raised. Grace thought Grandma Eliza's English accent was stylish and elegant. Grandma could also speak a little French too.

Grandma Eliza had died just about a year ago. Her family still greatly missed her, and the whole town mourned her too.

When Grandpa and Grandma Parfitt first arrived in New London from England with their young ones, they had lived in a log cabin. It was quite a change from the beautiful, large manor house where they'd lived in England. And instead of crossing Wisconsin rivers on arched stone bridges the bridge over the Wolf River "was made of broomsticks with ropes on the side to hang on to," Grandma Eliza often told them.

Grace would shudder, just thinking about crossing the river on such a flimsy bridge. "Didn't it swing in the breeze, Grandma?" she had asked.

Grandma had smiled, "Yes, that's why I dreaded crossing it. But in time I got used to it. It was the safety of my children that I worried about. The boys and Bessie thought it was great sport to cross that bridge. I just held my breath and prayed."

In her memory she could still hear Grandma's words and see her sweet face.

ELEVEN

The Autograph Book

When everyone had finished their last bite of cake, Mama pushed her chair away from the table. "Before we clean up, Grace, you should open your presents," she said. The gifts were stacked on a small table in the living room.

It was always exciting to open birthday presents, and wonderful to be the youngest in the family for everyone got something for her.

First Grace opened a red-plaid jumper from Daisy and a pretty blouse to go with it. The blouse had been Hettie's, but Daisy had easily adjusted it to fit Grace and even slightly changed the style. Mama had seen the plaid fabric at Milady's and could not resist buying it. "Grace has not had a new dress of her very own in a long, long time," she'd told Papa. It was almost a family project for Mama had crocheted a pretty lace collar for the blouse, and Daisy made the jumper herself.

From Bessie, Grace got a new pair of socks trimmed in red. They'd match the jumper.

Pearl's gift was a small book of poetry. Edwin gave her some brand-new pencils, and John presented her with a small, multi-colored rubber ball.

"After I helped old Mr. Wellington unload some boxes and put the goods on the shelves there at the general store," John explained, "he offered to pay me something, but I told him if it was OK with him, I'd just take the ball. I wasn't expecting him to pay me anything anyway. I just felt sorry for him when he fell on the ice and hurt his back last winter, so I helped him. His store is jammed with so much stuff. You know how he has floor-to-ceiling merchandise on nearly every square inch of wall space, with all those flatirons, stovepipes, saddles, teapots, and all. I figured he just needed help."

"That was commendable of you, John," said his mother. "I was proud of your generous spirit. Matt Wellington is not a young man anymore."

"I know. When he smiles, he shows more spaces than teeth," John replied with a laugh. "Anyway, Gracie, I figured you could use the ball to play jacks."

"You're right!" she exclaimed. "I surely do need a new ball. I think Bittie must have bit the old ball a couple times because it has teeth marks in it." She tossed up the new ball and caught it. "My ancient set of jacks must have come over on the Mayflower. Most of the paint is worn off, but that doesn't keep Margaret and me from playing with them. We love them."

"Actually," Bessie said, thinking. "I'm pretty sure that old set of jacks was mine."

"And before that they were probably mine!" added Pearl.

"Then you *did* bring them over on the Mayflower, didn't you, Pearl!" Edwin couldn't resist teasing his sister about her age, and Pearl was a bit sensitive about that topic. She'd never had a beau and somehow sensed herself as quickly becoming an old maid. So, of course, Edwin loved to hound her about being *elderly* every chance he got.

"Let's see," said Edwin with a frown as he playfully looked at the ceiling. "You went to school with Mrs. Jennings, didn't you, Pearl?"

"And you were in the class *ahead of us!*" Pearl replied with a grin. "Pshaw, age is not an important issue." With a twinkle in her eye she added, "Simply fib about your age and no one will ever know for certain just how old you really are." And that's what she did the rest of her life.

A comb and a new hair ribbon were Grace's gifts from Daisy. The red-plaid ribbon matched the red-plaid jumper.

"When I saw the bolt of ribbon come into the shop, I told Mama about it, and she said to get it for you," Daisy explained. "Mary Ellen tied it all fancy and fastened it to the comb so you can easily slip it into your hair. It will be especially nice if you pull your hair back. Come here, Gracie, I'll show you."

So Grace sat next to Daisy, while with a few strokes of the comb, Daisy placed the bow just so.

"Ooooo! Does that ever look nice!" Bessie exclaimed, and all the sisters agreed.

"I wish I had your hair, Gracie," said Bessie with a rather hopeless smile. "It adjusts so easily and your waves are so pretty."

"You hair is wavy, too. Well, sometimes, anyway," said

Grace trying to be generous. The family members looked at Bessie and grinned.

"But I have to use hairpins and crimp my hair in order for it to look like yours," Bessie explained. She shrugged her shoulders and smiled rather hopelessly.

The only remaining gift on the table was a small box. Grace opened it and found a small pair of shiny embroidery scissors. One handle was fashioned to resemble the head of a swan. The scissors were from Gustave.

"Oh, how lovely!" Grace exclaimed. She'd never seen anything like it. "Thanks, Gustave. They'll easily fit into my sewing box. They're so dainty."

"They match their lovely, new owner," Gustave said with a grin.

"Thank you, everyone." Grace's face and eyes gleamed. "All my presents are so nice."

"You're welcome!" they replied.

"Oops," said Papa in mock surprise. "See here. It's another present." And from behind his back he handed Grace a new jump rope with red handles that he'd fastened to the rope himself.

Grace's eyes lit up as she held the rope.

"Oh, Papa, it's great! I can't wait to use it. Thanks! Just wait till Margaret sees it."

"All right, girls, let's clean up," said Mama. "Boys, your father needs your help at the boathouse, and since it's your birthday, Grace, we'll excuse you from any chores for the rest of the day. Did you say Margaret was coming over?"

"That's probably Margaret now," said Hettie, hearing

a knock at the door. "Let her in, then go have fun. I'll put your presents away, Gracie."

Sure enough, it was Margaret, her eyes sparkling and her smile bright.

"Happy Birthday, Gracie Parfitt. Now we're the same age!" Margaret handed Grace a small present wrapped in fancy paper and tied with a bright ribbon. "This is something I know you've been wanting. Hope you like it!"

"An autograph book!" Grace explained as she unwrapped the gift. "Yes, I've been wanting one. Thank you!" She gave Margaret an impulsive hug. "Ever since you got yours for your birthday, I've had a hankering for one. Ooooo, it's so pretty."

The book was small with a soft, flowered cover, and it was tied with a ribbon on the binding edge. As Grace thumbed through the book, she noticed that Margaret had already signed the very first page and had drawn a heart in each of the four corners. It read:

> 2 Ys U R, 2 Ys U B
> I C U R, 2 Ys 4 me.
>   Love, Margaret Murphy
> P.S. Yours until Germany gets Hungary and
>   fries Turkey in Greece!

"Oh, Margaret! You're such fun," laughed Grace, and she turned to show the book to her mother.

"It's nice of you to remember Grace," Mama said. She placed her hand on Margaret's shoulder. "Would you like a piece of cake before we put it away? By the way, how's that mother of yours? I haven't seen her lately."

"Yes, I'd love some cake. You make the best cake in all New London, Mrs. Parfitt. And, yes, my mother's fine. She says to tell you that she hasn't forgotten your birthday's coming up this month, too."

Mama laughed. "I'm only two weeks older than she is, but she never let's me forget it. She likes to taunt me about being 'old,' bless her soul!"

"Gracie teases me, too, about me being three months older than she is. But I like being older. Then I can be the boss." Margaret turned to Gracie and made a funny face.

"Yes, you're old and bossy. Your face isn't wrinkled quite like Mrs. Jennings was yet, but it soon will be if you keep making faces at me," Grace retorted. Then deliberately squinting carefully at Margaret's head she said, "Hmmm, isn't that a gray hair, Margaret? Here, let me pull it out so that you won't grow more of them."

"Keep your pitiful, bony fingers away from my hair, Gracie!"

"But it shows, Margaret. That red hair of yours shouldn't be spoiled by a gray hair."

"My red hair doesn't mind a bit, and neither do I," Margaret laughed, wrinkling her freckled nose.

The girls loved to badger each other, but let someone else do it and there was immediate action. They guarded one another fiercely. Their mothers and their grandmothers had been friends from way back, so it was no wonder that Margaret and Grace were chums.

"I like the way you've done your hair, Gracie, and the ribbon is so fancy." Margaret obviously approved.

"Here, Margaret, have a piece of birthday cake," offered Bessie.

Margaret took the saucer and sat on a dining room chair. It was the last piece of cake, but Grace didn't mind at all.

Margaret glanced quickly at the gifts as Hettie stacked them up and put them away.

"Wow! Every present is nice. You're so lucky, Gracie," Margaret pouted with a funny smirk. "I have no sisters, and my brothers can't sew, knit, crochet, or even cook."

"Papa got me this new jump rope. Look, it has red wood handles. Leave it to Papa to be clever."

"Won't the girls at school be impressed? 'Specially, Lolly and Nola. We'll show them a fancy jump or two." Margaret's eyes twinkled merrily.

Grace and Margaret were the best rope jumpers in the neighborhood, and all the children knew it. On the playground at school, they were the jump rope champions, and no one ever even challenged them—especially not after the two of them had jumped the longest without missing a beat while Miss Simmons counted and timed them.

After Margaret finished her cake she and Grace went outside to play.

"Let's try jumping together. You take one handle, and I'll take the other, and if we stay close together, we'll fit side by side," Gracie suggested. They walk-skipped along in perfect rhythm saying:

"I asked my mother for fifty cents
        to see the elephant jump the fence.
I asked my mother for fifty more
        to see the elephant walk the floor.
He walked so slow he stubbed his toe,
        and that's the end of the wonderful show.

The next day at recess Grace took out her new jump rope. Tilda, Melissa, Corliss, and other girls in her class admired the new rope with the red handles and begged to have a turn with it. Grace was happy to share. "Corliss, let's do this alphabetically. Since your name comes first, you may have the first turn. If all of you will jump just 10 times, then everyone will get a chance before recess is over."

And that's exactly what the girls did. "Thanks, Gracie," each of them said.

"Your rope's the best on the playground," Margaret bragged for her friend.

When Lolly came along and asked for a turn, Grace's young heart wanted to say "no." But Mrs. Eldridge's words about the Golden Rule returned to her memory, so even though she felt uneasy about it, Grace handed her rope to Lolly. "Just 10 jumps, please, Lolly. That's what the other girls did."

Lolly quickly snatched the rope from Grace's hand, and swinging the rope with a swagger, she jumped 10 long, quick steps away from Grace.

"Hey, come back here!" called Margaret. "Don't you understand English?" Margaret ran to Lolly and grabbed at the rope.

Swiftly, Lolly pulled the rope back and replied, "Oh, I most certainly do understand English, Margaret. I only jumped 10 jumps, but now, of course, I'll have to deliver the rope back to Gracie, won't I?" And she quickly jumped 10 steps back to Grace, dropping the rope at her feet without so much as a smile or word of thanks.

"But that gave you 20 jumps, Lolly," Margaret said with exaggerated patience. "All the rest of us did 10 just as Gracie asked." She was livid.

"Goes to show you who's clever, *don't* it, Margaret," said Lolly with a haughty smirk.

"You can't even use good English, Lolly!" Margaret hollered as Lolly took Nola's arm and quickly skipped away. "She's a brat," grumbled Margaret.

"Yeah, she's a big brat," said the girls.

Grace picked up her rope and changed the subject. "I'll bring my long rope tomorrow, and we can do California Oranges. Won't that be fun?"

At supper that night Grace told her family how Lolly and Nola had pushed their way into her game. "They always seem to get the upper hand," she said, "and it really isn't fair."

"If I'd a-been there, I'd have walloped Lolly a good one," John loyally declared, a defiant lift to his chin.

"No, that's not the way. Don't be upset by ill-mannered playmates, and don't try to match wits with them on the playground either." Mama's voice was soft but composed. "The place to match wits with anyone is in the classroom. Give them a run for their money in your studies, and don't let them earn an easy "A." You might be surprised and get an "A" yourself."

The children laughed. "You're right again, Mama," Edwin cackled with his mouth full of popcorn.

"Well, Lolly isn't a top-notch student, so I'll have no trouble there. But she is hard to beat in a fight," Grace said with a downcast look. "Usually Lolly and Nola don't bother with us anyhow."

"Be friendly to them, anyway, and ignore their high-falutin' ideas," was Hettie's advice.

"Margaret and I try to be friendly, but they don't seem to notice."

"And the more offended you act, the more they'll put on airs."

"Wel-l-l," pondered Grace. "They usually run around with the Lolly's older sister, Dovey, and her friends."

"Humph," grunted Hettie, "they have a rather high opinion of themselves, so don't let them bother you, Gracie. They probably figure that it gives them prestige to be seen with older girls."

"Pres . . . what?" Gracie wondered.

"Their social standing—that being with the older girls makes them better than their classmates. It really doesn't. Lolly's wrong. She and Nola will have their comeuppance someday, and they'll have to pay the piper. Don't pay attention to their conceit." Hettie always knew now to console her little sister.

"You're a comfort, Hettie. I wish I could be popular like you," Grace sighed. "You'll be a great teacher." Hettie was in high school and very well liked. Everyone knew Hettie, and everyone loved her. She planned to go to Normal School in Waupaca and get certified in elementary education. Both she and Edwin planned to become teachers.

"Just relax, little sister," Bessie said with a smile. "Popularity is a very fickle thing anyway. Overnight it can vanish into thin air. If it's any comfort, I think you're wonderful!"

Mama looked at Grace and her heart hurt because Grace was distressed. "My dear young daughter, arguing gets one nowhere. Always remember that the Bible says, 'Don't fret yourself because of evil doers.' And Jesus also tells us, 'Blessed are the peacemakers, for they shall be called the children of God.' Keep in mind those texts."

"Did you have squabbly girls around when you grew up, Mama? I can't see that anyone could be worse than Lolly Jones and Nola Hampton." Grace frowned just thinking about them.

"Oh my, yes," Mama laughed. "In this life you'll often have difficult people to deal with." She laughed. "Oh, I remember Nettie Cameron. That girl was a thorn in my flesh when I was a child, but she grew up to be a nice, mature woman. Her husband died young, leaving her with four small children, and I felt sorry for her."

"Humm," Gracie murmured. It was hard to think of Lolly and Nola as grown up even though they thought they already were grown.

"Of course, I always had Lucinda Kelly as a forever friend just as you have her daughter Margaret. I'm glad the Murphy's have remained close to us through the years." She paused. "As far as the playground is concerned, Gracie, there's an easy way to control the jump rope."

"But how?" Grace couldn't imagine an easy answer to her problem. "When we're jumping with the long rope, she just comes up and jumps in real quick like."

"Tell you what, my girl, everyone needs to learn the lesson of ownership. When you see Lolly coming and about to jump in front of someone, you, as owner, have the right to stop the turning. Put out your hand and grab the rope. In fact, if you are one of the turners, immediately pull the rope taut. There'll be no way anyone can jump rope when the rope itself creates a barrier. Then quietly ask Lolly to go to the end of the line, and tell her you'll be happy to let her jump when it's her turn. She'll get tired of bullying when she finds she is unsuccessful in her attempt to intrude. Of course, that doesn't guarantee that she'll immediately turn into a pleasant, mannerly girl."

Papa couldn't help but grin.

"My good wife, for as peace-loving a woman as you are and how you like to foster goodwill, you amaze me at your cleverness!"

Again the laughter around the table was cheery.

"I remember you giving me that advice, too, Mama, when I was Gracie's age," recalled Bessie. "I think growing up is about the only solution sometimes. It just takes time, but it's hard to be patient when you're a kid."

"Well, children, listen up," said Papa. "People are people. Some give us joy when they greet us, and some give us joy when they leave us." The children laughed, and he continued, "Don't let others determine your behavior or your self-image. Be your own person."

"Sometimes I think boys have it easier than girls do," said Gracie. "John and Edwin never seem to have trials with their friends."

"Boys may not be spiteful like girls, Gracie," said her father, "but they, too, have their tussles with bullies. I remember my little brother Austin, having to struggle with that rascal Jeremiah Phillips. But when we finally convinced Austin to stand up to him, the battle was won.

"Jeremiah was larger than Austin but one day when he said to Austin, 'So, you want to fight?' Austin put up his fists. He stepped right up to Jeremiah and boldly looked him in the eye, then asked 'Ready?' Jeremiah was dumbfounded. He stammered something and walked away, and all the other boys started to laugh. A fight never took place, and Austin became much more confident after that." Papa gently smiled, but his eyes filled with tears. It wasn't often that he spoke of Austin.

TWELVE

Lightning
Always Wins

Tonight when Grace went to bed she had the room and entire bed to herself. Pearl had gone to stay with Annie for a few days, to help out. It was still a while before the baby would come, but Annie needed help with spring housecleaning and with taking care of Dell.

Grace wouldn't have minded going too, but especially she liked having the bed to herself. She could sprawl spread-eagle, stretch in any direction, or sleep crosswise if she wanted. So she flopped this way and that. She heard her mother's footsteps on the stairs then down the short hall. Before going back down, she peeked in on Grace to say goodnight. Grace waved her mother into the room.

"I've been thinking," she began a little hesitantly. "Will you tell me about Uncle Austin, Mama? I've heard bits and pieces from Papa or others about an accident, but just how did the accident happen? I think I'm old enough to know. Will you please tell me the whole story?"

So Mama sat on the edge of the bed and took Grace's hand. Then she began:

"Your Uncle Austin and his wife Mary—her name is Mary Millicent; isn't that a pretty name? Well, Austin and Mary bought a home out on Huntley Road near us and your Parfitt grandparents. Your uncles Joe and Jim and their families were very near too. We were all on the same road.

"Just a short time before, we had all put lightning rods on our houses. Everybody was talking about the necessity of doing so. So your father reminded Austin that he should put up lightning rods on his house, too. Immediately! Austin said that he'd do it the next day but that tomorrow came and went.

"One day your father stopped by to see Austin. Papa said that the children came running to meet him. He picked up little Janie and swung her around. Cally proudly brought out their new wagon for his 'Unka Henry's' inspection."

Grace giggled at that. Little children were so cute. Maybe Annie's new baby would call John "Unka John."

"Well, Cally and Ivrin showed him how high they could go in the swing your Uncle Austin had hung in a nearby tree," Mama continued. "Austin and your father had a good visit, and before Papa left to go home he reminded Austin to put up lightning rods. He was especially concerned because Austin had strung a wire clothes line from a big tree all the way to the corner of the house. Papa and Austin hugged and said goodbye." Mama smiled, but she looked sad, too. "You know how men hug and slap each other on the back. I can just see Papa and your Uncle Austin doing that. Austin said to tell us all hello. It was just a normal visit, but that was the last time your father saw his kid brother alive."

Grace gasped, listening wide-eyed as her mother went on.

"A terrible storm came late that night, and lightning struck the tree where Austin had hung the clothes line. Tragically, the wire line was a much better conductor for the electricity than the tree was. The discharge zoomed down the wire and into the house. The lightning made a hole in the wall as large as a man's hand. I saw it later, and I was shocked. The metal bed was toward the wall, and the electricity struck Austin in the back of the head. It passed through his body from head to foot. He died instantly. He was only 32 years old.

"Your Aunt Mary was lying next to him, and the lightning burned a lock of hair off one side of her head and left a mark under her shoulder. She was completely stunned for more than a half hour afterward. Then she regained consciousness and recovered her speech."

By now Grace was sitting up in bed against her mother, her face buried in her mother's neck. She almost wished she hadn't asked about this, for as Mama told the story Grace could almost see it happening all over again.

Mama's arms were around her, and she buried her face in Grace's hair. Neither of them spoke.

"Then what happened to Aunt Mary?" Grace whispered.

"Aunt Mary was expecting a baby. The poor baby was born a few days later, but it didn't live more than a day or two." Mama kissed the top of her head with a sigh. "Now, precious, that's the complete story. Your papa still feels the sorrow over losing his brother."

Again they sat on the bed in silence. Grace brushed tears from her eyes.

Downstairs they could hear Papa's footsteps. He was probably checking the house, closing it up for the night.

"You lost a sister once, too, didn't you, Mama?" Grace asked in a small voice.

Holding her close, Mama nodded in the pool of light from the kerosene lamp. "Yes, I lost my only sister, your Aunt Annie Laurie, when she was just a young mother. She had married your Uncle Jim, and they had two little boys, Rollie and Harry. Harry was only two months old when she passed away.

"By the way, did you know that Rollie and Harry are your *double* cousins? Yes, ma'am, they are because two of the Parfitt brothers married two sisters—me and Annie Laurie. Our children are doubly related. Isn't that nice?"

Grace had heard snatches of the story before, but now she had been told the complete version by her own mother. "Life just isn't fair, is it, Mama? Bad things happen for no good reason," she said seriously.

"No, honey, life isn't fair. But always remember that when we experience tragedy God is sad along with us. We live in the land of the enemy, and sometimes must live by Satan's rules. However, the apostle Paul tells us that we do not need to mourn as those who have no hope."

"I know!" Grace's voice was excited. Here was a burst of light in the darkness of these two sad deaths. "Paul says that there's going to a resurrection, and we'll see Aunt Annie Laurie and Uncle Austin and Grandma Eliza and . . ."

"Oh, *yes!*" Mama breathed. "We'll be reunited with our loved ones and Christ, Himself, will take us to heaven to live with Him where there is no more death. That gives me a lot of comfort."

"That's what I've heard Pastor Morrison say, but now it makes more sense to me," Grace said. She gave her mother another hug, then slipped out of her arms and under the bedcovers. "Thanks, Mama. Goodnight." She looked up and smiled.

"Goodnight, my little one. See you in the morning. Sleep well." Mama kissed her daughter on the cheek and blew out the lamp.

THIRTEEN

Crown of Ivy

A few days after the unhappy playground episode, Grace and her friends were jumping with the long rope. Grace and Margaret were turning the rope while the others jumped in one at a time. They all chanted:

> "California Oranges,
> Tap me on the back!"

When the words "tap me on the back" were repeated, the next girl in line had to jump in without missing a beat and tap the current jumper out. Each girl then returned to the end of the line. If you missed the beat, you were "out." When everyone had jumped, then different girls would turn the rope and a new line formed.

Sure enough, Lolly and Nola casually walked by, trying not to look at the jumpers. Then in a flash, Lolly turned and ran toward the rope. Grace and Margaret were prepared. They pulled the rope up tight just as Lolly ran forward. She was stopped dead in her tracks.

Dumbfounded, Lolly said, "Think you're smart, don't ya?"

"Smarter than you are, Lolllllyyyyy!" Margaret smirked.

G-4

97

"You may go to the end of the line and take your turn if you like, Lolly," said Grace.

Still somewhat bewildered, a puzzled look on her face, Lolly defiantly walked away. Corliss and Melissa grinned at Grace. Tilda said softly, "It worked."

Yes, indeed. Grace thought to herself. *Doesn't matter if Lolly and Nola are such pests. They don't have the sense God gave a goose. Anyway, Miss Simmons says we usually learn more from our enemies than we do from our friends.*

It was hot. Flowers, vegetables, and weeds grew in abundance. The garden needed tending, and the children pitched in to help, although there was some grumbling about it. It was much more fun to play than work, but they all knew they must carry their share of responsibility.

One Sabbath afternoon, Mama attended a Sabbath School Council meeting in the park near the church. Mrs. Eldridge asked Grace if she would come and help to entertain her granddaughter, Annabelle, for the hour or so during the meeting. Annabelle was 4 years old, and she was visiting her grandmother. Grace agreed. She had met the little girl before and liked her. The child was sweet and playful.

Grace sang songs and told stories to help entertain Annabelle, but the little girl's interest faded fast. So Grace walked around the park with her, looking at birds and flowers. Then for a while they sat under a tree, and Grace picked and wove a garland of ivy.

Placing the circlet on her own head, Grace grinned at Annabella. "How do I look?" she asked.

Annabelle's big hazel eyes sparkled. "Just like Queen Esther."

When the council ended and folks prepared to return to their homes, Mrs. Eldridge thanked Grace for her help. "You were a blessing," she said. "I'll remember you for your kindness."

"Bye, Gracie. Come over to see me right away," called Annabelle.

Grace smiled and waved.

When they got home, Grace and her mother sat on the porch and enjoyed the sunshine. Tip and Bittie joined them. Grace petted each of them, and Tip gratefully licked her hands and gave her face a gentle kiss.

Grace woke early the next morning scratching vigorously. Her arms and face felt like they were burning with fire. One look in the mirror told her she was in trouble.

Pearl and Bessie were helping their mother prepare breakfast, and Grace ran to them crying with pain.

"Gracie, what has happened?" Mama asked.

"I don't know. All I know is that I itch."

"Oh, dearie, I wonder if you got into some poison ivy yesterday in the park," Mama said. "It looks like you have a rash on your face."

"On my arms, too," Grace almost cried. "I must have braided my garland from poison ivy. What a miserable crown it turned out to be!" She slumped into a chair and buried her swollen face into her swollen hands. "Look, I'm broken out all over!"

Bessie ran for the Calamine lotion and began dabbing and covering Grace's face and arms. Then they saw spots of rash on her neck, and chest, and legs. She was covered with a raw, red rash. All Grace wanted to do was go back to bed, and Mama agreed that was probably the best place for her.

Poor Grace hardly remembered the rest of that day or the next. Mama had the doctor come to see her, for she was *sick*. After examining her, he said that the rash was even in Grace's mouth and under her eyelids. Her eyes were all but swollen shut. He suspected that the poison ivy was affecting her inside as well as out.

Mama tried bandaging her up like a mummy, but Grace just couldn't stand it and ripped the bandages off. To Grace it seemed like a bad dream that lasted an eternity. She lay in a haze, only aware of the itching and the pain. In the next days she barely remembered her parents and brothers and sisters speaking quietly to her when she was awake. She told them to go away. It was too painful to even hear them talk. She was sick to her stomach and wanted nothing to eat. Bessie sat by the bed and nursed her gently and faithfully, rarely leaving her side.

When at last she sensed some relief, her sisters brought cool water and mild broth to drink. Light oatmeal gruel appealed to Grace, and Bessie fed it to her by the spoonful. Normally, gruel was not Grace's favorite, but somehow it appealed to her now.

"You'll make a wonderful nurse, Bessie." Grace whispered her thanks and weakly smiled.

Slowly, she began to recover. When she finally felt strong enough to get up and out of bed, her legs felt like wobbly noodles. She laughed at herself, and Edwin came to help her down the stairs.

"Easy does it, little sister," he said kindly. "Do you want me to carry you?"

"Oh, no," Grace replied, "I'll make it."

Carefully, she crept into the living room and eased herself into a chair. The sun was bright. Neighbors were in their yards and walking down the street. A whole world was going on outside the window, but she didn't feel like joining it.

John brought Tip and Bittie to her, and she enjoyed that.

Soon she was ready to go back to bed. Edwin walked with her up the stairs. She was glad to lie down again. But every day she grew stronger, and it seemed that in no time at all she was back to her normal self. She was ready for company.

Grace looked forward to Margaret coming to visit. "Want to go out and sit in the grass and look for four-leaf clovers?" Margaret asked with a mischievous grin.

"I want nothing to do with clovers or weeds for a long time!" Grace laughingly replied. And never again did Grace knowingly touch poison ivy.

FOURTEEN

Cave-in!

 August brought not only heat but humidity. It seemed to make folks irritable.

"Great Scott. It's hot!" complained Edwin. "Give me chilling winds, icicles, snow, and blizzards to this depressing heat." Both he and Grace enjoyed winter. They never minded the cold, even when the temperature was below zero.

One sultry morning Margaret joined Grace sitting on the back porch in the shade.

"What shall we do, Gracie?" she asked. "I know, let's play hopscotch."

"Naw," replied Grace, "let's swing. At least we'll be in the shade while we swing."

"But we swing lots of times, and I say let's play hopscotch," Margaret insisted.

"Hopscotch takes too much jumping around, Margaret. I'm not in the mood to move much."

"Well, you have to move when you swing. You have to pump your legs!" Margaret declared just a little louder than she needed to.

"But swinging makes a breeze!" Grace snapped. "And I don't want to hop around like an idiot in this heat."

"If that's how you feel, Gracie Parfitt, I'm going home!" Hands on her hips, Margaret spat out the words with a dark scowl.

"Why? Just because I don't want to move around?" Grace's voice was even louder than Margaret's.

"We play hopscotch lots and lots of times," she continued, talking fast. "We're always playing what *you* want. Right now *I* want to swing in the shade. Maybe later if it cools off we can play hopscotch." Grace stamped her foot in exasperation.

"You think you always get to choose what we're gonna play. Well, today, I'm gonna choose, and I say we play hopscotch! So there!"

"Well, Miss Bossy, I'm not gonna play hopscotch! Why are you so cranky and stubborn today?"

Grace ran the back of her hand across her forehead. She felt hot, sweaty, and irritable. The girls rarely fought, but this was one of the times they did.

"I'm not cranky. I just won't be bossed. I'm so mad I'm gonna go home, and I'm not coming back, Gracie, until you are *hungry* to see me." That was Margaret's favorite expression when she was really upset.

Off she went in a huff, her red braids bouncing with each determined step. Grace shrugged. She knew she wouldn't probably see her friend the rest of the day, and she regretted that.

I should have compromised with her and suggested something else. Oh well, she'll feel better later, and so will I. We never can stay mad with each other for very long.

103

Each girl was stubborn. That was a fact.

"I never saw the likes of you two," Edwin laughed as he came from the shed. "You both are as hardheaded and obstinate as the other. But I've seen you when you're with the other kids at school, and you're like thick and sticky glue. Nothing pulls you apart!"

"That's the way we want it," was Grace's resolute answer.

"No one gets the best of you—unless it's you, your-selves, right?" Edwin needled.

Disgruntled Grace went into the house. She dipped herself a glass of water from the bucket on the sink then sat down in a chair. The sky was clear, the sun was hot, but still it was a beautiful day. In her heart Grace wished that Margaret were with her, even if it meant having an-other game of hopscotch.

Grace remembered how Margaret came to visit when she'd been so sick with poison ivy. Bessie said that Margaret had come by several times to see how she was, and she came to visit the very minute Grace felt like hav-ing company. *Hummmmph!* Grace thought.

Bittie jumped into her lap and meowed softly. Grace gathered the calico cat in her arms.

"Bittie, you're *always* agreeable. You don't argue or sass anyone." Bittie purred loudly at the sound of her voice and the gentle touch of her hands. "Oh, how you love to be petted, you beautiful thing. Cleopatra herself couldn't have been more attractive than you are."

Grace had learned a little about the Egyptian queen at

school. "Cats were very popular in Egypt, Bittie. If you had been a royal cat, you could have floated down the Nile River with the queen in her own private vessel and had your own private birdie-stew to eat at dinner time." Bittie pushed her head into Grace's hand, asking for more petting.

Grace carried the cat to the porch where she sat down, leaning against the wall of the house. She still felt out of sorts, but Bittie's loving purr had made her feel better.

The afternoon dragged on. Mama had her come in and grate cabbage for slaw and do a few other things to help with supper. Grace was glad when the day was over.

"There was a tragic accident down near the cheese factory where men were digging trenches for the water and sewer pipelines," Papa told them during supper.

Instantly, everyone's eyes were on him. Grace felt her heart jump to her throat.

"Whatever happened, Henry? Tell us," Mama urged.

Papa's face was sober. They could tell he was upset.

"A cave-in." His voice was barely audible. "Two men involved."

"Oh, Henry," Mama was immediately sympathetic.

"A cave-in, Papa?" Grace's eyes were wide with fright.

"Did someone get killed?" John asked, as his sisters echoed his question.

"Yes," Papa sighed. "Someone was killed. I didn't know the man. They said he was from Tigerton."

Everyone sat in stunned silence.

Grace heaved a sigh of relief. "I'm so glad it wasn't Mr. Milliken."

"So am I. He's the one who is safely alive. But it was touch and go they tell me."

Grace's hand flew to her mouth. "Oh, how Corliss must be feeling."

Papa slowly buttered a thick slice of bread then cut a thin slice of cheese. He took a sip of buttermilk then placed the cheese on the bread and took a bite.

"As you know," he said, clearing his throat, "all the workers are warned to be on the alert for possible cave-ins. It's a rare thing, but if the soil or weather conditions are right, that is a real danger."

"But digging's got to be done," Edwin asked. "Right? The town needs running water and sewers and such."

Father nodded soberly. "Of course, Edwin. And we're proud of the progress being made here in our own town. I, for one, am glad to see it. But there's no doubt about it, it's dangerous work. The trenches have to be deep enough to be below the frost line. Otherwise, come winter, the pipes would freeze, and no one would have running water. At any rate, all workers are told that if they hear or feel the slightest rumble they must stop digging and run or climb as fast as they can! We've all heard the stories of men being covered so quickly by a cave-in that they can't get away fast enough. Either they're bent over as they work, or their feet get caught, or they're knocked down and not able to jump up or escape."

"Just like Mr. Cornwell, huh, Papa," said John in a whisper.

He nodded. "But this man from Tigerton was not as fortunate as Walter Cornwell. Anyhow, the two men caught by the cave-in were completely buried. Their co-workers heard the commotion and began digging furiously at the spot where they felt the men would be. Almost immediately, one fellow who was digging and prodding with his bare hands saw a slight movement of dirt, so he yelled for more help and kept digging frantically."

Mama stood up and paced the floor.

"Henry, I can't stand it," she cried. "Hurry with the story!"

"Well, immediately this fellow saw part of a man's head. It turned out to be Mr. Milliken. They dug all the more furiously hoping to free him before he smothered to death. Harley Milliken later told the workers that his whole body was held fast and he could barely breathe. But for some unknown reason he could move his head slightly. So when he heard muffled voices through the dirt, he quickly blew air from his mouth and tried to yell. The movement in the dirt may have been what caught the diggers' attention. Harley's convinced his guardian angel protected him, and nobody can persuade him any other way. I agree."

"Will he be OK?" Grace whispered.

"Yes, I believe so. Dr. Pfeifer was called immediately and took him to his office. He told us that it was only providential Harley is alive."

Edwin dropped his fork on his plate with a clatter. "Who'd want a job like that? There are better ways to earn a living!" he declared.

"That may be true in your opinion, Edwin, but the public works men obviously don't feel that way. Not everyone wants to farm, you know. I didn't. But accidents occur on farms, too. Every occupation has risks of some kind. You remember that old Mr. Compton was smothered to death in his own haymow," Papa reminded them.

"Yes, and Juby Mitchell died when he got gored by a bull," said Daisy.

Grace instinctively put her hands over her ears.

"Buried alive. . . . Imagine what a story Mr. Milliken can tell to his grandchildren," Hettie said.

Everyone silently agreed.

It was a quiet group that took their dishes to the sink and went to their different chores for the evening. Grace dried the dishes, handing them to Edwin who put them in the cupboard. She felt warm and happy toward him. He was a good brother, even if he had teased her about her spat with Margaret. Her serious mood followed her onto the porch that evening. Mama sat in the wide-armed rocker fanning herself with a newspaper. The air had cooled slightly, but Tip panted where he lay at John's feet.

Night was falling. Lightning bugs flickered on and off under the large, leafy trees. Grace smiled to herself, thinking of how she and her brothers sometimes caught the bugs in a jar and tried to use their light to read by. Then she giggled aloud, remembering how she and Margaret used to love running among the "lights" when they were younger.

FIFTEEN

Making Up

In the morning, Grace awoke to another warm and muggy day. After breakfast, she decided it was time to mend her fences with Margaret, so grabbing her rope with the red handles she skipped down the street, saying:

"One, two, buckle my shoe.
Three, four, shut the door.
Five, six, pick up sticks.
Seven, eight, lay them straight.
Nine, ten, a big red hen!"

Margaret saw her coming and waved. "Hi, Gracie!"

"Hi, Margaret." Gracie panted a little as she ran toward Margaret's front porch. "Can you come over to my house, or maybe I should say *will* you come over to my house and play? I'm sorry I was short tempered yesterday."

"That's what I like about you, Gracie. Your folks named you right. You always know how to be *gracious*." Margaret grinned. "I was the one who started the tiff."

Grace trotted up the porch steps and playfully tugged on one of Margaret's braids. "I'm sorry," she whispered.

"Me, too."

Just then Margaret's mother opened the screen door. She had a dust cloth in her hand.

"'Morning, Grace," she said brightly. "The house gets so dusty these hot days," she said, stepping to the far edge of the porch and shaking it vigorously.

Grace returned her greeting then asked, "Mrs. Murphy, is it OK if Margaret comes over to play?"

"Please," Margaret said.

"And while I think of it," Grace added, "would it be OK if we went over to see Corliss? You heard about her father's accident at the cave-in yesterday. I'm glad he's alive, but we could tell Corliss that we're glad he's alive, too, and have been thinking about her."

"She must have been awfully scared when she heard it," Margaret put in.

Mrs. Murphy gave the dust cloth one last shake. *It's wonderful how quick the girls are to make up,* she thought, but she didn't say anything about it. Instead she smiled. "Certainly, Gracie. It's nice of you to think of Corliss. Do greet your mother for me, too."

The two friends had grabbed hands and were dancing around the porch. "Margaret,"—her mother grabbed her hand and for a moment the three danced in a line—"be sure to be home before noon."

Off the girls scampered. First they stopped and told Grace's mother where they were going. Then they were off for the Milliken home. By the time they reached Corliss' house they were breathless. They knocked gently at the door, and

Corliss opened it. She stepped out quietly to welcome them.

"We just came to say that we're sorry about your father's accident, and to see how he is, and to see how you are, too," began Margaret.

"He says that he's pretty sore all over. We all know just how close we came to losing him." Corliss' sweet but sober face reminded them of the seriousness of the accident.

"All of us have prayed for all of you, Corliss," Grace told her, "and we thanked the good Lord that you still have your father. When everything has settled down, come over and play with us."

"We'd like that," Margaret added. "Grace and I could stand a little change in our conversations, huh Grace?" Her eyes crinkled in the corners as she smiled.

"We sure could, Corliss," Grace agreed. "Come any time. It really isn't that far to Oshkosh Street."

Grace twirled her jump rope, and Corliss reached out and grabbed it in mid-swing. Grace let go of one handle. Corliss slipped her hand up to take the other handle, and they began expertly turning the rope in high loops.

Without a word Margaret jumped into the rhythm. "One, two, buckle my shoe. Three, four . . ."

Margaret ran out, circled around Corliss, then ran back in. None of the three missed a beat. "Five six, pick up sticks . . . Nine, ten, a big red hen!"

Margaret ran out again. "Corliss, do you want to jump next?" she asked.

She shrugged. "I don't know. Do you want to jump next, Grace?"

Grace dropped her end of the rope. "Not particularly. You take the next turn."

Quickly, Corliss and Margaret traded places. The rope beat the packed dirt on the path, and Corliss ran between its beats.

"One, two . . ." She dipped and touched the ground between jumps. They chanted the numbers rhyme twice then easily slipped into:

> "Teddy bear, Teddy bear, turn around.
> Teddy bear, Teddy bear, touch the ground.
> Teddy bear, Teddy bear, shine your shoes.
> Teddy bear, Teddy bear, read the news.
> Teddy bear, Teddy bear, go upstairs.
> Teddy bear, Teddy bear, say your prayers.
> Teddy bear, Teddy bear, turn out the light.
> Teddy bear, Teddy bear, say good-night!"

Without missing a beat Corliss did the action that each line described. At last, red-faced and laughing she stopped dead where she stood.

"Oh! That was *fun*," she gasped. "Thanks so much for coming over."

They agreed to meet later that day and Margaret and Grace waved goodbye. The walk home was warm and humid. When they got to Grace's house they immediately went to the back yard and took long, cold drinks from the squeaky hand pump. Tip heard the water running, so he crawled out from under the back porch where he'd tried to stay cool. Grace continued to pump so he could snap off bites of water from the down-pouring stream. He was good at this doggie-drinking process, and the girls laughed and enjoyed watching him. Grace filled her hand and sprinkled Tip with a spray of water. He looked up, gratefully wagging his tail.

She patted his head and said to him, "I'm surprised you're not with Papa, Tip old boy. Why aren't you down at the river with him? You usually follow him everywhere, but maybe he told you to stay home this morning."

Everyone in the family loved Tip, but he was definitely Papa's dog. They were constant companions. Papa had picked him from a litter of pups born on Uncle Joe's farm. From the beginning, Papa said that he was the smartest dog he had ever seen.

"Let's have Tip do some tricks for us," Margaret said.

Papa had trained Tip to allow a small piece of cheese to be placed on his nose without moving his head or blinking an eye. Only when he was told, 'OK, it's paid for,' did Tip toss his head, making the cheese fly up in the air. He'd catch it on the way down and eat it.

Grace shook her head. "It's too hot today, even for dog tricks. I think I'll not bother him. But Papa has taught him a new trick, and I tell you I simply could not believe it when I saw him do it yesterday."

Tip sensed they were talking about him, and his tail began to wag as he rolled his eyes up to Grace.

"That's right, Tip, you are such a smart doggie." Grace scratched him behind his ears. "Papa says he thinks you get just as much fun out of doing tricks as we do watching you!"

"What's his latest accomplishment, Gracie?"

"Well, you know that Papa and Mr. Leuwek are friends," began Grace.

"You mean the chief of police?" interrupted Margaret.

"Ah-huh, the chief himself," nodded Grace. "Well, Papa has taught Tip to play dead. Tip will drop to the floor and never moves a hair. Then Papa tells him real excited and quick like, 'Beecher Leuwek is coming!' and Tip scrambles up and races into the other room fast as he can go. It's so funny, we all burst out laughing. You'd think he was afraid for his life—that the police were on his trail!"

Margaret laughed and scratched Tip's head. "You funny dog!" she told him.

"Toward evening, Papa took him down to the station where Mr. Leuwek was still working. Edwin, John, and I went along, and Papa had Tip do the trick. Mr. Leuwek laughed so hard he doubled over.

"He told Papa he had one smart dog, and that people can tell the mettle of a man by his dog. I never thought of that before, but I don't know of a person in town who hasn't heard of Tip and his owner."

Margaret nodded, still scratching and petting Tip's head. It was just too hot for anything. She reached over and pumped the pump handle up and down again, bending over for another cool drink. Grace stretched. Tip ambled over to the shade of a nearby tree.

The squeak of the screen door told them that it had opened.

"Oh, hi, Hettie, come join us," Grace called. It was

Hettie who'd just stepped on to the porch. She smiled at the girls, looked at the sky, then said, "Muggy, isn't it. But I guess we could use a good rain." Then she went back into the house.

In silent agreement, both girls went to sit on the porch steps. The air was heavy and still. Muggy! Hettie was right. Margaret giggled. "Muggy" was a funny word, but maybe it described exactly how you felt. Hot and damp all over. Itchy too. She lifted her skirt above her knees so her legs would get a little more air. Even the bees seemed to buzz lazily as they flitted from flower to flower. After a while, Margaret said, "Let's go down to the river and see if your father is back yet with the boat. Besides, it might be cooler near the water."

During the summer Henry Parfitt owned and operated an excursion boat, the "Little Steamer," on the Wolf River. Margaret was fascinated with the boat and was always thrilled to be invited for a ride. At that moment she was thinking that nothing could be nicer than to have a boat ride to cool off. But Grace was not fond of boating at all—it made her seasick. She liked the river better in the winter when it was frozen solid, and she could ice skate on it.

So with some effort, they lazily got up and strolled down to the river with Tip at their heels. Sure enough, by the time the girls arrived, Grace's father and John were coming out of the boathouse. Apparently they'd just put the boat away, and Margaret was disappointed.

SIXTEEN

Tornado

"Hello there!" As usual, Papa greeted them with a smile. "Is it hot enough for you?"

He wiped his forehead with a damp handkerchief and looked up at the dark clouds that were beginning to gather over the town.

"I'd say we're in for a good storm," he observed, shaking his head. "You girls had better head for home or you'll get caught in a downpour. Gracie, tell your mother I'll be home very soon. I don't like the looks of that sky. It's tornado weather."

Suddenly, Grace felt scared. She didn't much like storms. And now that Papa had mentioned it, the sky was a funny gray-green. And the hot, heavy air was so still.

"Let's go!" she cried, and the girls raced down the street. But before they could get home the wind picked up. It felt good to them—cool—but within seconds it was whipping dust and leaves and small sticks against their bare arms and legs.

Suddenly large drops of rain began to fall. It was strangely cool and very windy. Wild, dark clouds hovered on the far horizon, and a bright flash of lightning ripped across the sky. Then the girls heard a low rumble of thunder. The storm was coming nearer. Even as they ran, they kept nervous eyes on the heavy sky.

Waving goodbye to Margaret, Grace skipped up the back porch steps, glad to be home. She almost bumped into Hettie who—hands on her hips—was frowning at the threatening sky. Good-natured, fun-loving Hettie was not very good-natured or fun-loving when it came to storms. Like Grace, she just hated them!

"Papa said to tell you he's on his way home with John. He fears a storm is coming," Grace told her mother.

"And I fear he's right," agreed Mama. "Be a good girl and help Edwin close all the windows so it won't rain in. And tell your sisters it's time to stop sewing and come down here."

Daisy, Pearl, and Bessie were upstairs in their bedroom. They'd just stood up to put away their things and come downstairs when Grace walked in.

A sudden booming crash of thunder and bolt of crackling lightning sent Grace and Edwin flying down the stairs. In that moment, Papa and John with Tip burst into the house, the wind loudly banging the door behind them. Their rain-soaked shirts clung to their bodies.

"It's frightful out there, Marilla!" Papa told her. He looked worried. Hurrying to the stairway he called, "Everyone come down here immediately!"

Daisy and Bessie needed no urging but instantly obeyed, jumping several steps at a time. As usual, Pearl stubbornly dilly dallied and took her time.

Papa quickly ordered everyone into the dining room

and instructed them to stay away from the windows. Going again to the stairway he shouted, "Pearl, I mean NOW!"

The wind began a high, whining roar in the trees, and the bushes in front of the house lashed about frantically. By then the wind was blowing so fiercely that the family could feel the walls of the house trembling. Pearl appeared instantly.

Rain beat fiercely against the windowpanes. It seemed that every moment brought the flash and sizzle of lightning with cracks of thunder behind each flash. The wind moaned in fury.

Grace was afraid, deathly afraid. She closed her eyes, covered her ears, and stood numb and paralyzed. For how long she didn't know. She couldn't move. Never before had she experienced such a wild storm. Wave upon wave of rain pelted the windows. Lightning seemed to tear into the room, flashing, roaring, crashing. How long would this go on? There seemed no sign of lessening. Huddled against her parents, she cringed and shuddered. Was this all just a bad dream?

Suddenly Grace knew full well why her father was extremely cautious about lightning. Its strikes were filled with power. And in a heartbeat the whole story about Uncle Austin flashed through her memory.

"Don't ever underestimate the power of lightning, children. When lightning strikes, lightning wins!" In her mind she keenly remembered her father's warning words.

How she found herself in her father's arms, she did not know. He held her tightly in one arm, and his other arm was wrapped securely around her mother. Grace leaned heavily against him, burying her head on his chest. He was shaking. Edwin and John sat huddled in a corner with their heads between their knees. Tip was pressed against John's leg. Daisy and Pearl hid under the table with Bittie. Bessie and Hettie hugged tightly right next to Grace.

The next crash was so close and deafening that Grace felt she would faint. Her whole body slumped as she looked up into her father's ashen face. His eyes searched the ceiling as he mouthed the words, "Dear God, please." She knew immediately that he was praying for the safety of their family.

Then a gush of roaring, raging wind shook the kitchen. There was an awful sound of shattering window glass and breaking wood. Overhead they heard shingles ripped from the roof. Then with a terrible, splintering *whoosh*, a rushing, deafening blast of howling wind roared into the dining room. Part of the kitchen roof had been lifted right off the house and blown apart!

From somewhere in the dark, rain-whipped room a small voice called, "Papa, Mama; are we all right? Are we all here?"

Grace hardly knew that she spoke. The darkened room, the shrieking wind . . . everything seemed unreal.

"Is it over?" Bessie was barely able to whisper. "What shall we do?" she asked. "Oh, what shall we do?"

John reached over and touched Tip's head. Only then did the dog whine.

No one moved. They just listened. *What would happen*

next? Minutes passed. Papa still clasped his youngest child against him, his other arm cradling his wife. The rain continued, though, perhaps, not quite as hard. Thunder rolled across the sky, but maybe it was a little further away.

After what seemed like an eternity, the storm was over. The family gasped, blinked, and looked at each other. Daisy and Pearl crept out from under the table. Bittie mewed piteously and jumped from Pearl's arms. The storm was over. No one was hurt.

They almost stumbled into each other as they trouped into the kitchen and gaped at the huge, ragged hole in the ceiling. They could look through the hole in the roof right up at the clearing sky.

Grace and Bessie ran outdoors.

"Papa, Mama, come quickly," they called.

Papa could hardly believe his eyes. Some of the backyard trees were uprooted, and their chicken coop had been blown into the neighbor's yard. Providentially, nothing more serious had happened.

The children walked aimlessly, shaking their heads, picking up bits and pieces of things the wind had blown into their yard. It was hard to tell how things had been—before the storm. Papa put a protecting arm around Mama, and they stared at the devastation in disbelief.

Then Papa softly said, "Well, Mama, we have a lot to be thankful for. We're all safe and sound." And he quoted a verse from Psalm 91: "He shall give His angels charge over thee to keep thee in all thy ways."

Mama wiped her eyes with the corner of her apron. Now that the storm was over she let herself shed a tear. "Come, everyone," she said briskly. "Let's get busy."

Papa and the boys immediately took over. Someone went after the ladder. The others found something with which to cover the hole in the kitchen roof. It would do until the roof could be repaired. In the house, Mama and the girls picked up broken glass, and more glass, and then even more! Once they'd carefully picked up the large pieces, there seemed no end to the razor-sharp small fragments.

The table had been overturned and the tablecloth had been blown against the wall where it stuck tight like wallpaper. Two chairs were broken, and the stovepipe was knocked down. Soot and water covered everything like mud. They mopped and sopped up the kitchen floor, dumping out pail after pail of water.

"It'll take forever to clean this place, Mama. Whatever will be do?" Grace asked as she looked up to the damaged roof, then around the room.

"It won't take forever, Gracie my dear, but I fear it will take weeks to get everything back to normal." Mama calmed her youngest and smoothed the hair from her flushed forehead. "Come, let's sit down a minute."

Big as Gracie was, Mama pulled her to her lap and they sat for a moment, just catching their breath.

Every now and then another neighbor brought tiny, soaked chicks to their door. Though the poor things had been blown here and there, none seemed badly hurt. The neighbors stayed to describe the damage done to their own properties, wagging their heads in astonishment at how quickly the storm had blown into town and how completely unprepared they'd been.

"Sounded like a train of cars rumbling along," declared one.

"I never heard the likes of it!" remarked another.

"It blew our shed to smithereens," a little boy announced.

Everyone agreed that it was a wonder that no lives had been lost.

Of course, the Parfitt's were anxious to know how the rest of their big family had fared during the storm. During the next day or two they were thankful to learn that though every home had some serious damage, no one had been hurt.

By nightfall, Gracie's family had cleaned up much of the mess caused by the storm. Before they went to bed, Papa led them in thanks to their Heavenly Father for protecting them during the storm. From Gracie to her father, each of them knew full well that unseen angels had watched over them that afternoon. They had truly been sheltered in the shadow of the Almighty.

Before crawling dead tired into bed that night, Grace knelt beside her bed, weary but not too weary to pray and give God her own personal word of appreciation.

Thank you, Father, for taking care of us today. You hid us under Your wings, and Your feathers covered us. You were our shield or we would not have survived. May I always re-member how we were preserved in the hollow of Your hand, and may I ever serve Thee. Amen.

Even when she was an old lady with grandchildren of her own, Grace never forgot that frightening storm. In years to come, she and Margaret spoke of it often, and so did everyone else in New London. Many years after this storm, Grace repeated the story to her own children.

Other storms in other years came and went, but none of them was as fierce or as damaging as the tornado that tore a hole in the kitchen roof.

The Rest of Grace's Story

Grace grew up to be a slender, trim young woman who easily arranged her brown curls into the popular hairdos of the day. The name Grace seemed to describe this rather quiet, gentle miss who moved with dignity. With her slim figure and natural poise, she wore clothes well. Her brother-in-law, Charles Bowyer, Bessie's doctor husband, said of her, "When Grace dresses up she looks like a million dollars!" Throughout her life, both in posture and presence, she was truly graceful.

Young Grace was delighted when Annie and Reynolds named their baby daughter Marilla Grace. She enjoyed her visits to Annie's—holding the baby and playing with young Dell. Three years later Daisy and Gustave named their first baby Grace. So while she was still young, the Grace of our story had two namesakes. Her sisters, indeed, cherished and treasured their little sister and wanted her memory to live in on the names of their children.

Sadly, while Grace was still in school, her mother suffered a stroke. It left Marilla only slightly paralyzed but without the ability to speak. To help herself walk around the house, she used a light-weight chair as a cane. She could help do the dishes by washing and rinsing with one hand. Unfortunately, it eventually became necessary for Grace to take over the housekeeping duties, and she reluctantly dropped out of high school.

While still young, Grace had learned to cook and bake bread. Now she became an expert at baking apple pies, and they became family favorites. Her brothers bragged about her delicious apple pies, and she was often asked to bake a pie or two whenever the family got together.

As time passed, Grace became more and more efficient at keeping the house clean and running smoothly. Her father often complimented her on this. Unable to speak, her mother would smile and silently nod in agreement.

Grace remained at home, taking care of the house and her mother until Marilla's death. By now Grace was 26 and may have wondered what she was going to do with her life. Here Bessie and Charlie stepped in. They invited her to come live with them in Milwaukee and attend business school. This program was open to those who had not finished high school, and Grace jumped at the chance! In exchange for her room and board, she helped care for the three Bowyer children. Bessie was delighted to have her "little sister" near her again.

The Bowyers loved singing in the Milwaukee church choir. During choir practice one week a call was made for volunteers to assist a young minister who'd come to town to pastor the Italian mission. He was going to hold evangelistic meetings. Charlie offered to help lead the singing at the meetings, and Bessie willingly played the piano.

They both were impressed by the pleasant, talented, bilingual evangelist with the lovely tenor voice.

When Bessie came down with a cold, she asked Grace to take her place at the piano for the next evening or two. And that's how Grace met the young, single pastor, Justus Vitrano, who politely rode home on the streetcar with her that night after the meeting.

After that, Grace played for many of the meetings. Her friendship with the pastor grew to courtship, then marriage. Her wedding attendants were, quite naturally, Bessie and Charlie. Daisy, Grace's seamstress sister, made her wedding gown. It fit perfectly.

Grace was a true helpmeet to Justus. She played the piano for church services and, much to the delight of their church members, sometimes sang duets with him, too.

Exceptionally organized and creative, she used these abilities in leading out in activities for the church's youth. She planned interesting Sabbath school programs and Friday evening Missionary Volunteer meetings. She sponsored Junior Missionary Volunteer classes where children earned honors in many different categories. Her joyful enthusiasm helped them take pride in being invested as Friends, Companions, Comrades*, and Master Comrades. In heaven's books Grace's legacy may well be recorded as a faithful Christian woman, wife, sacrificial mother, and teacher.

Grace and Justus had three children: Genevieve Marilla, Steven Parfitt, and Ruth Elizabeth. You will meet Ruth in Book 4. 🌐

---

* Now called Guide and Master Guide

More About Grace's World— a World of Change

Grace was born into a world of horse-drawn wagons. By the time of her death, spaceships had circled the earth and men had walked on the moon.

By 1900, when Grace was 10, there were only 8,000 cars on all of the roads in America. Telephones had been invented, but only 1 in 13 homes had one. Only 1 in 7 homes had a bathtub. There were no radios or electric ice boxes.

Grace liked to say that their childhood home had running water. "We ran to the well and pumped it!" she'd laugh.

Women did the family washing in tubs that were hauled into the kitchen using water that had been heated on the coal or wood-burning stove. Depending upon how dirty they were, clothes were soaked, scrubbed, and rinsed several times, then boiled, starched, wrung out, and hung to dry. Each change of water had to be hauled inside and heated on the stove. No wonder it took all day to do the laundry!

In 1903, Americans made their first airplane flight.

In 1903, Henry Ford helped begin Ford Motor Company.

Ice was cut from frozen lakes and rivers then stored in sawdust in huge icehouses. Old Cyrus, the ice cutter, would have worked— or perhaps supervised—a team of men who used special tools to cut the river ice and haul it away for storage.

In 1900 the life expectancy for white women was 48.7 years; for non-white women, 33.5. For white men it was 46.6; non-white, 32.5.

There was no vaccination for diphtheria or typhoid and these, along with malaria and pneumonia caused a lot of deaths. Houses were heated by a stove or fireplace and the heat didn't circulate to the bedrooms. A heated brick wrapped in flannel was good for warming icy feet in an icy bed.

Grace: 1890-1973

Inventions that changed Grace's world

1898: typewriter
flashlight (called "an electric hand torch")
1901: the first radio transmission
1904: the first tractor
1907: plastic
1911: home refrigerator—made available by General Electric; invented by a French monk
1913: the modern zipper
1921: insulin. Now rather than facing certain death, diabetics could live healthy lives.
1927: TV. Its inventor, Philo Farnsworth, was only 20 years old. The first all-electronic image was a simple black line.
1929: penicillin

And just for fun

1900: toy trains, invented by Joshua Lionel Cowen
1902: the Teddy bear
1903: crayons

The Adventist Church in the early 1900s

1899: Christian Record Braille Foundation opened.
The first conference-wide youth organization was created at the Ohio camp meeting. It was called Christian Volunteers.
1903: The world headquarters of the SDA church moved to Washington, D.C.
1907: Creation of the Young People's Missionary Volunteer Department. Its three major aims were to help kids develop their devotional life and to promote missionary activities and educational activities.
1910: College of Medical Evangelists (now Loma Linda University) opened.